At the Edge
of Our Longing

D1531272

Other Books by James Conlon

Geo-Justice: A Preferential Option for the Earth
Earth Story, Sacred Story
Lyrics for Re-Creation: Language for the Music in the Universe
Pondering from the Precipice: Soulwork for a New Millennium
The Sacred Impulse: A Planetary Spirituality of Heart and Fire

James Conlon

At the Edge of
Our Longing

Unspoken Hunger for Sacredness and Depth

NOVALIS

© 2004 Novalis, Saint Paul University, Ottawa, Canada

Cover design: Caroline Gagnon
Cover image: Getty Images (Digital Vision)
Layout: Christiane Lemire, Francine Petitclerc, Richard Proulx

Business Office:
Novalis
49 Front Street East, 2nd Floor
Toronto, Ontario, Canada
M5E 1B3

Phone: 1-877-702-7773 or (416) 363-3303
Fax: 1-877-702-7775 or (416) 363-9409
E-mail: cservice@novalis-inc.com
www.novalis.ca

Library and Archives Canada Cataloguing in Publication

Conlon, James, 1936–
    At the edge of our longing : unspoken hunger for sacredness
and depth / James Conlon.

Includes bibliographical references.
ISBN 2-89507-522-0

    1. Spiritual life. I. Title.

B105.S64C65 2004   204'.4   C2004-904288-2

Printed in Canada.

We acknowledge the financial support of the Government of Canada through the Book Publishing Industry Development Program (BPIDP) for our publishing activities.

5 4 3 2 1 08 07 06 05 04

Acknowledgments

I would like to thank the following people, whose support, friendship and good work made it possible to bring this project to publication: Cara Anaam, Sallie Goetsch, Joan LeFlamme, Cynthia Trenshaw, Marilyn Goddard, and Jane Heckathorn.

Michael O'Hearn, Kevin Burns, Anne Louise Mahoney and Danylo Dzwonyk of Novalis.

Also the faculty and students of the Sophia Center in Culture and Spirituality at Holy Names University in Oakland, California.

And each of you who experience the longing of soul, life, Earth and divine.

Table of Contents

Introduction

I am fascinated by the title of this book. It evokes several connections with what modern scientists call "the edge of chaos" which does not describe the onset of chaos but its after-effects. Chaos theory describes a state of internal dislocation, because the old certainties don't make sense anymore. The order begins to disintegrate, disorder ensues, and the system veers toward a freshly discovered sense of coherence.

This is the edge of chaos. The old will never be the same again, but the new is still unfolding, sometimes confusing, chaotic, stretching, even exciting. It is not neat and precise like the old order, but intuition tells us that it is a great deal more real, and this is what compels credibility.

Jim Conlon brings a creative and intuitive mind to this "edge of our longing," but he goes beyond the *longing* into the realm of *belonging*. And the *belonging* is no longer just personal, interpersonal or social. It is planetary, global and cosmic. This is Conlon's revolutionary insight. Moving through the four spheres of Soul, Life, Earth and the Divine, the psychologist within me hears resonances of stages of developmental growth. The difference, of course, is that these are planetary/cosmic stages and not merely personal ones.

This is precisely what the edge of chaos is about. The previous, familiar world of conventional wisdom no longer holds. The certainties crumble, the clarity fades, the boundaries are stretched, often beyond recognition. We are into new territory: disturbing, dangerous, challenging, but for growing numbers among us, exciting and promising. Assuredly, we have been there before, and nobody knows the territory better than the mystics both ancient and recent. Jim Conlon graciously acknowledges their enduring contribution.

But even for the mystics there is a radical newness. We encounter a new evolutionary movement that is beginning to dawn upon our world. None of us has been there before. We need fresh wisdom for our time and for our journey. You would be advised to take along a copy of *At the Edge of Our Longing*. You'll find it a useful resource, solace for the turbulent times, guidance at the crossroads, and above all reassurance for the different future that embraces our world in these opening decades of the 21st century.

Diarmuid O'Murchu
June 2004

At the Edge of Our Longing

God speaks to each of us only in making us
And then walks silently with us out of the night.
But the words before our beginning,
cloudy words, are these:

"Sent out by your senses,
Go to the edge of your longing,
Give me something to wear.

Flare up like a fire behind all things;
So that their shadows expand
to always cover me fully.

Let everything happen to you: Beauty and terror.
Just keep going: No feeling is the farthest out.
Do not let yourself be parted from me.
Near is the land
which they call life.

You will know it
by its earnestness.

Give me your hand."

—Rainer Maria Rilke
(translation by Br. David Steindl-Rast, OSB)

Prologue

As Bruce Springsteen says, "Everybody's got a hungry heart."

Our days are marked by many cultural signposts – globalization, the information highway, a propagandized media, political disenchantment, questionable elections, pre-emptive wars, economic downturns, despair of the youth.

We live in a world that seems bent on its own destruction, that has abandoned its wisdom sources and the healing power of intimacy and contemplation in relationship to soul, life, Earth and the divine.

It is a world where planes become weapons, classrooms become war zones, and wars break out in Afghanistan, Iraq and the Middle East; a world where the innocent ones and the beauty of creation are sacrificed on the altar of global unrest.

We live in a world that is marked by a new age of anxiety whose defining moments are terrorist attacks and homeland security; a world where reverence for the child as the icon of hope has been squandered through acts of kidnapping and abuse.

A world where the vision of a better tomorrow has collapsed in daily reports of global conflict, ecological degradation manifest in extinction spasms, poisoned water, toxic air and land, the interspecies spread of diseases like SARS and monkeypox, the pandemic of HIV and AIDS, and battles over oil.

A world where participation in the Great Work, humanity's historical mission, has been reduced to monitoring economic indicators and regular visits to the mall.

In the words of Rainer Maria Rilke I discovered a title for these pages and a spiritual strategy for responding to the dislocation that many of us experience today. I suggest that it is by reflecting on and responding to our experience of longing that we will develop a spirituality for living in and transforming today's world. Longing is a theme that permeates our cultural soul. We are being invited to remain balanced in our quest for intimacy and contemplation.

Through intimacy we commune deeply. Relationships become the monasteries where we deepen our discovery of meaning and purpose. Through intimacy we fall in love with soul, life, Earth and the divine and embrace fully the joys and sorrows, beauty and pain of existence. Our experience of intimacy will be complemented by our experience of contemplation, liberation and creation.

In contemplation we embrace silence and stillness; we quiet the mind and penetrate the fault lines of the psyche; through intimacy we gain fresh energy and move forward to heal a broken world.

When our experience of intimacy, contemplation, liberation and creation is understood within the context of the universe, we are transported from any tendency to self-centredness and enter into a world that is vast and cosmic. This journey of solitude and communion will move us forward into new frontiers of sacredness and depth.

As we embrace the balanced experience of intimacy and contemplation within the context of the universe, we cross the threshold into a mystical cosmology of sacredness and depth; we find an engaged spirituality whereby we become one with our soul, with life, with creation and with the divine. When intimacy and contemplation is viewed from a perspective that integrates quantum physics, evolutionary science, psychology, theology and cultural analysis it culminates in an approach I now call Engaged Cosmology.

It is my hope that mystical and Engaged Cosmology discovered from experiencing the longing of soul, life, Earth and divine can become a spiritual resource whereby we view our life in the larger cosmic context and feel a healthy sense of responsibility for the planet.

As we listen and "get a glimpse of the cosmic dance" (Merton), we realize that our longing "echoes the divine longing" (O'Donohue).

Nourished by the realization that we are engaged in a spiritual journey named by the poets, lived by the prophets, and revealed by the universe, we move forward to heal and transform the world.

In our longing for sacredness and depth we explore and experience the

- Soul, in those contemplative moments that touch the heart and prompt us to change and grow.

- Life, through opportunities to transcend anxiety and become liberated from everyday confusions, to embrace relationship and wisdom.

- Earth, in communion with creation as the source and sign of ecological harmony, balance and peace.

- Divine, as the vulnerable and receptive one, calling us into relationship and into the experience of contemplation, liberation and creation, inviting us to belong and instilling in us the courage to confront the challenge of the day.

At the Edge of Our Longing: Unspoken Hunger for Sacredness and Depth is an invitation to embark on a common journey to melt into our consciousness a cosmic awareness that draws courage from each other and enchantment from creation as we open ourselves to the surging miracle of life.

Guardians

I swear I will not dishonour my soul
with hatred but humbly offer myself as
a guardian of nature
As a healer of misery
As a messenger of wonder
As an architect of peace....

I want to know if you know how to melt into that fierce heat of living
falling toward the center of your longing.
                  —David Whyte

The Genesis

A prophet combines a very deep love, a very powerful dissent, a
powerful resolve with envisioning hope.

—Rabbi Abraham Heschel

The genesis for a mystical and engaged cosmology was born in me when I envisioned what would be an ideal sabbatical; my plan (yet to be realized) was to visit the people and locations where the most significant and prophetic spiritual work was being done. It consisted of exploring three theological approaches and subsequently to create a synthesis of these three when viewed from the context of the new universe story.

I would begin by spending time at Gethsemane Abbey near Bardstown, Kentucky, and during my visit spend time with the work of Thomas Merton; I had been there in 1965 when Merton was alive. It seems like yesterday, as I recall the celebration of the feast of Corpus Christi at the Abbey. The monastic cloister was carpeted with petals as we slowly processed with the monstrance containing the host in gratitude for the gift of the Eucharist. Intuitively, I knew then, and now more vividly, that the contemplative life at Gethsemane provided an opportunity to pay attention to the presence of God and explore the deeper recesses of my soul, and the interdependence of all things, within the Catholic tradition into which I was raised.

Somewhere I knew, as the Buddhists say, that "action without prayer is a fragile thing." I knew that the contemplative journey is necessary – if we as a people are going to be able to engage in the great issues of our time (race, gender, class, health, war and peace, ecological devastation) and confront the dark night of our cultural soul that so permeates this moment. Merton wrote in his final book that the "inarticulate longing for him in the night of suffering will be your most eloquent prayer"; with these words he named my experience and the experience of many of us today, "The Longing of Soul."

The next step on my "ideal sabbatical" was to go to Peru to visit the Institute of Bartholome de Las Casas and Gustavo Gutierrez, the recognized father of Liberation Theology. In Latin America and among oppressed peoples around the world (South Africa, Brazil,

Asia and more), liberation theology has stirred a fresh energy among people committed to freedom, dignity, destiny and fulfillment. Gutierrez describes the liberation process as the commitment to "think through our faith, to strengthen our love and to give reason for our hope." He reminds us that the experience of oppression is incompatible with the Christian tradition, that faith and life are inseparable. He states that liberation involves freedom from death – a death that is both physical and spiritual – and demands access to food, housing, health care, education, workers' rights, employment, and self-expression in both politics and religion. Liberation is guided by the principle of the "preferential option for the poor." With this in mind we acknowledge the presence of divinity among those "lowest on the social ladder," the most abused of society. We also realize that the fullest experience of liberation has three important dimensions: freedom from internalized oppression (intrapsychic), freedom in relationship to others and the structures of society, and freedom in our relationship with the divine. I realize now that liberation theology contains a response to the question "What is my response to the Longing of Life?"

The third moment on my sabbatical journey was to take me back to the Riverdale Center for Religious Research for conversations with Thomas Berry and to the Learning Center at Genesis Farm in New Jersey where, with Miriam MacGillis, OP, and her colleagues, participants are invited to explore the new cosmology and its implications for our lives. I hoped that this period could include conversations with Thomas Berry, Rosemary Radford, Brian Swimme and others, as well as the possibility to read and reread their work. The appropriateness of this component, "The Longing of Earth," is found in the words of Thomas Berry: "There is, in a sense, a new revelatory experience that has given us a new sense of the universe, a new sense of the planet earth, a new sense of life, of the human, even a new sense of being a Christian. We have, in a sense, a new revelatory experience through our present understanding of the time-developmental universe." As we view the world through the lens of creation theology our perception of the world is transformed; we go beyond soul and life to include our relationship with the natural world. When the sun greets us each morning, the kitten warms itself by the window seat, the clouds choreograph the sky, and the mystery that envelopes us as dusk guides us onto the threshold of night, we have entered the world of creation theology. We realize anew that "a fully healed, liberated person also means a healed and liberated earth." We experience each expression of creation as sacred; we are bathed in the wonder and awe of creation. The words of Hildegard of Bingen take on new meaning: "Every creature is illuminated by the brightness." With this in mind we celebrate the whole world as sacrament, with humans as interdependent members of the earth community collaborating fully in its future and well-being. Upon reflection it has become apparent that the genesis of a mystical and engaged cosmology is aligned to the principles of the cosmos. In this way contemplation is related to interiority (sentience and spontaneity), liberation to differentiation (unending variety), and creation to communion (everything is related) – each interconnected within the context of the universe itself.

The fourth chapter, "The Longing of the Divine," is the culmi-nating section of these pages. Here we re-vision each of the previ-ous chapters (soul /contemplation, life /liberation, and earth /cre-ation) from a new cosmological perspective. In the "Longing of Soul" we understand the psyche (soul) to be co-extensive with the uni-verse. In the "Longing of Life" we extend our view of liberation to embrace the entire earth community, including every species. In the "Longing of Earth" we celebrate a sacramental consciousness that sees each moment as revelatory. We gain access to fresh psy-chic energy and a new awareness to move forward to create and transform the world. "Longing of the Divine" becomes a synthesis of contemplative liberation and creation theology within the con-text of the universe itself. With this in mind we move forward to participate in an engaged cosmology and create a strategy for a just and peaceful world: a world of geo-justice where the dynamics of the universe become a template for harmony, balance and peace; a world of engagement where the wisdom and practice of cultural workers of yesterday and today can become empowered by the universe to fashion a new creation and heal the face of the earth.

My Second Exodus

As I reflect on my current interests, I realize that we have amongst us today people whose work continues to embody the hoped-for result of my sabbatical. With the contemporary contributions of Br. David Steindl-Rast, OSB, Albert Nolan, OP, Brian Swimme, Rosemary Radford Ruether, and Thomas Berry, the resources and desires that I wanted to pursue in far-off places are with us and their work is available and present.

However, an exciting new dimension has been added: contemplation, liberation and creation are now gathered together into a seamless garment of consciousness and set in the context of the cosmos. In connection with this integration, Rosemary Radford Ruether writes, "Each of these spiritualities not only have their distinct validity, but also continually interact in new and creative ways." It is the interaction of these spiritualities in their cosmic context that takes us to the threshold of mystical and engaged cosmology. As architect Richard Register writes, "Engaged cosmology should mean taking action in the physical/social world congruent with lessons from evolution and ecology."

Longing pulls us down into our own depths as we become more open to the World.
> —Susan Plummer Freeman

Without the in-breath of self-care and reflection we can't sustain our involvement with the suffering world…without the out-breath of compassionate engagement with society our inner work implodes upon itself leading to the dead end of narcissism and spiritual emptiness.
> —Gail Straub

To call out of the future the longed-for present.
> —Walter Wink

Deep within the heart there is the primal pain of longing, the cry of the soul separated from its source. The pain comes from the memory of when we were together with God. This process allow us special moments in our life when we can taste of this union, a taste of the divine remembrance.
> —Judy Schroeder

*The problem is how to remain in the midst of the distractions of life;
how to remain balanced, no matter what centrifugal foreces tend to
pull one off center.*

—Anne Morrow Lindbergh

Longing is the core of mystery.

—Rumi

In a Dark Time

*In a dark time, the eye begins to see
I meet my shadow in the deepening shade
I hear my echo in the echoing wood...
What madness but nobility of soul
At odds with circumstance?
The days on fire!
I know the purity of pure despair...
The edge is what I have.*

—Theodore Roethke

Longing

*Delicate enough
to pass unnoticed
as air,
as shadow
as light
as idea,
that's how I long to be*

—Julia Esquivel, V.

1

Longing of Soul

Canticle to Soul

Let us

- give voice to our unspoken hunger, to our quest for sacredness and depth
- keep on believing in the fruitfulness of our efforts
- join with those who are willing to risk their lives and lifestyles that others may flourish and live
- become sensitive to the poverty of the planet and listen to people in pain
- nurture new expressions of compassion and co-create structures of peace
- become fully present to those we love
- nurture a new spirituality to energize a world of harmony, balance and peace
- celebrate Earth as a living community and our common home
- practise non-violence and celebrate each moment as an epiphany of kindness, beauty, listening and love
- remember our story and let go of anything that stands in the way of living fully with a listening heart

- search for the subtle presence of the divine, especially in the cry of the poor who allow the divine to shine through
- search for sacredness and depth, where the unspoken hunger reveals the language of connectedness, cosmology and soul

And we will discover who we really are.

Moments of Sacredness and Depth

Longing of Soul/Contemplation

Contemplation and Soul: Reflection

Soul happens in relationship, in moments of intimacy and of solitude. As we remember incidents of depth, experiences touch the heart and our spirit soars. We imagine healing all separateness and are embraced in the genuine depths of compassion, home, silence, friendship and inclusion. Soul becomes a compass of hope.

No one has changed a nation without first speaking to its soul.
—Robert Bellah

Soul is fundamentally a biological concept, defined as the primary organizing, sustaining, and guiding principle of a living being.... The universe and the human soul find their fulfillment in each other. Soul gives to the multitude of living forms wondrous powers of movement and reproduction, but even more wondrous powers of sensation and emotion.... The entire universe is shaped and sustained in all its interwoven patterns by the mysterious powers of soul.
—Thomas Berry

The Longing of Soul can be best understood through the lens of contemplative theology. Here we focus our conscious attention on the presence of the divine in all things; as we respond to the longing of the soul we integrate our experience through a deeper awareness of the interior life and the mystery of existence.

Contemplation literally means putting together according to some measure... contemplative life is the putting together of vision and action. Vision alone is not true contemplation. We must put vision into action.
—Br. David Steindl-Rast

Contemplation is the keen awareness of the interdependence of all things.

—Thomas Merton

The contemplative has broken through to that sanctuary in the soul where love dwells.

—John O'Donohue

This mystique of ethical commitment is accompanied by a mystique of contemplation.

—Leonardo Boff

Interiority links the psyche of individual human beings to the timeless force of God's spiritual reality.

—McGregor Smith

Contemplative spirituality seeks to unite the "soul" with the permanent source of reality.

—Rosemary Radford Ruether

The story of the evolutionary universe opens the door to understanding the possibilities of the contemplative life because the realization of the "fullness of the present now" is the core of contemplative life.

—Mary Coelho

Soul in the context of the new universe story refers then to the unseen, self-organizing, shaping dynamism of the person.

—Rupert Sheldrake

Soulwork is inner work, either personal or collective, which nourishes our capacity to experience connection and interdependence.

—Community Action Network (CAN)

Dublin, Ireland

To live a contemplative life is to be open enough to see, free enough to hear, real enough to respond.

—Marie Beha

What is madness but nobility of soul at odds with circumstances.

—Theodore Roethke

To be a contemplative we must become converted to the consciousness that makes us one with the universe.

—Joan Chittister, OSB

Contemplation is a secret, peaceful and loving infusion of God, which if admitted will set the soul on fire with the spirit of love.

—John of the Cross

Could the universe have a soul, and are we that soul with the entire cosmos for a body?

—Ernesto Cardinale

The contemplative gaze renders the whole world sacramental.

—Elizabeth Johnson

Soul is just the way black folks sing when they leave themselves alone.

—Ray Charles

The planets correspond, then, to deeply felt movements of soul.

—Thomas Moore

I began to think of the soul as if it were a castle made of a single diamond.

—Teresa of Avila

Her image had passed into his soul forever and no word had broken the holy silence of his ecstasy.

—James Joyce

Reflection: In contemplation we commune with cosmic forces, with ultimate mystery; we practise a spirituality born out of the depths of the universe in moments of intimacy and solitude.

Contemplation and Soul

God's presence alive within
Even in the leaf God is there.
There are so many mysteries
The tiniest little creatures of nature
Teach us all to be grandmothers and grandfathers
Everything is relationship and holy awe

A Sabbath for the Soul

May I be at peace
May my heart remain open
May I know the beauty of my true nature
May I be healed.

—Morningstar guidelines for soulful living

Constantly regard the universe as one living being,
having one substance and one soul.

—Moses Hadas

Our souls are shaped by stories – stories we hear and stories we tell ourselves. Those narratives give shape to who we are in our own eyes. They also name the sequence of events that tell others about us, and identify who we are to the world.

A primary threshold to freedom is telling our story differently: to include our accomplishments and emerge from the closet of self-deprecation, to transform a self-taught litany of failure into a banquet of blessings, to announce our presence as an unexpected moment when grace entered our lives and provided in the midst of turbulence a Sabbath for the soul.

A Sabbath for the Soul

Deep within the restless world
resides a profound pursuit
an uncommon quest
for intimacy and rest

A longing for peace
relief for the journey
a relentless pursuit
a search for oneness
a loving embrace

that heals the heart
is balm for the soul
that longs to just be
and experience there

A Sabbath for the Soul

These moments of Sabbath and rest happen when the longing of the soul is quenched and we are one with our heart's pursuit.

These mystical moments heal the heart and envelop us in a mystery that alters and illuminates our lives.

Moments that bring to mind the beauty of the stars, the trajectory of a swallow in flight, the arching leap of a pickerel from silken waters as the sun recedes in the west.

Moments in the backyard with your baseball coach as you listened eagerly to his reflections on the game of life.

Moments of portent and prophecy while following in the footsteps of Martin Luther King, Jr. on Woodward Avenue in Detroit, Michigan, when your heart opened and imagination soared to embrace the social gospel as a vehicle to alter and illuminate our lives.

Moments when, after years of study and reflection, mystical and engaged cosmology becomes more than words; when suddenly, as if for the first time, we become one with the star, the sunset, the bird, the fish, the mentor, and see in each the God who came down from heaven and in each "a Sabbath for the Soul."

The mystical is not how the world is but that it is.

—Wittgenstein

Being Selected:
The Closing of the Prison Door

The capacity to listen and respond with an open heart reveals much about ourselves and our capacity for generosity and compassion.

This incident, which was told to me by an Irish official, occurred when the inmates of Mount Joy Women's Prison in Dublin, Ireland were being transferred to a new facility. It is a story that reminds each of us of our need to be chosen, to be recognized, to have our value acknowledged. This need for respect sometimes shows up in unpredictable ways.

On Christmas Eve, during the closing of the women's prison in Dublin, an older female prisoner stepped forward and declared to the man in charge, "I want to close the door for the last time!" When he asked why, she declared, "I have the right – my grandmother was here, my mother was here, my sisters were here, my baby sister was born here and I'm here!" Following her plea, she was selected to close the door for the last time.

At the new prison after the liturgy on Christmas Day, she clung to a photo of her closing the door and walked around showing it to everyone present. It was a sad yet powerful moment. On a day for remembering the birth of the liberating Christ, she was proud of being selected to close the door to the prison that had housed the women of her family over so many years. She challenges us to cultivate a willingness to listen with our hearts, to accept the humanity of the other – her value, experience, wisdom, pain and unrealized potential – to discover and experience satisfaction by bringing hope, contentment and appreciation of the other.

Prisoners are often looked upon as dangerous and damaged – people without status, esteem or respectability. It is so important to listen to people at the bottom, to realize that each of us in our way is "doing time," each of us imprisoned in the cellblock of internalized oppression, the iron cage of the system that lives within.

> *Whoever you are, no matter how lonely, the world offers itself to your imagination, calls to you like the wild goose, harsh and exciting, over and over answering your pleas.*
>
> —Mary Oliver

Grace Happens

Grace happens when we explore the deep inner currents of belonging and realize the profound connection between our aspirations for life and the concrete requirements for living.

Grace happens in possible and sometimes impossible ways.

Grace happens when our mood shifts and we discover new people and projects in seemingly mysterious ways.

Grace happens when we discover anew that life has its own trajectory and that we know deeply that we live in a universe where we are not in charge.

Grace happens when we discover that life requires effort, effort in what often feels like effortless ways.

Grace happens when we work hard, stay focused, yet realize the outcomes are far beyond our awareness, energies or control.

Grace happens as a gift, a manifestation of an unfolding universe whose ultimate trajectory is always toward the good.

Grace happens when life becomes embedded in mystery and surprise.

Grace happens when we awaken to many questions and are willing to remain uncertain yet in pursuit of the quest.

Grace happens when in our soul-searching we find a way to heal the wounds of childhood.

Grace happens when science speaks to us and reveals its many patterns on our path.

Grace happens when in the midst of our search we discover that place of hope where our secret longings lie.

Grace happens when in our restlessness we discover colleagues in pursuit of justice who also long for a life of harmony, balance and peace.

Grace happens when we discover at the threshold of unexplored frontiers a quantum realm wherein reside the secrets of what it means to be alive.

Grace happens when we embark anew on a journey to celebrate fresh expressions of wisdom, to see each expression of creation as a unique manifestation of sacredness and new life.

Dispelling the Darkness

"It's already dawn."

—John XXIII

Winter solstice has a profound impact on our souls. On the shortest day of the year darkness permeates the earth; it is a time when we pause to consider how events of our day spread fear and terror across our darkened land.

I think of an elderly woman from Jerusalem sitting at her kitchen table on the first day of Hanukkah anticipating the next terror attack. Meanwhile a child plays in Baghdad and pleads with her parents to stay up late to play a game because she fears that soon another bomb will drop and there will be no tomorrow.

Here in Berkeley more than 2,000 people crowd into the high-school theatre to remember and celebrate the life of Father Bill O'Donnell. Father Bill's very existence was dedicated to dispelling the darkness of injustice.

Winter solstice is the time when the sun begins to return to Earth, a powerful symbol reminding us of the Son of God coming to Earth on that first Christmas.

At Christmas God leaves the remote recesses of the divine light and shines instead into the dark lives of the marginalized and victimized.

—Leonardo Boff

Dinner with Donna at Christmas

Hospitality is the way we turn a prejudiced world around, one heart at a time.

—Joan Chittister, OSB

It was Christmas morning in Brielle, New Jersey. Outside the winds sent blistering sheets of rain across the windows and into the streets. Snow was promised by the forecasters as people in this village on the Jersey Shore and other coast-side towns prepared to stay inside away from winter's fury on this day on which we celebrate a child's birth.

The doorbell rang; my sister and I welcomed my sister's friend Fran and her friend Donna to our newly formed Christmas Day community. Fran is a volunteer with the Association of Retarded Citizens (ARC) and had chosen to share the holiday with Donna, a developmentally challenged adult, and with us.

Donna's presence among us turned out to be a gift, an "unexpected incarnation" on that Nativity morning, encouraging us to reflect in a new way on the meaning of the day and what it is that we, in fact, celebrate on Christmas.

As I entered into Donna's obvious enjoyment of her Christmas lunch, I found myself musing on Christmas and its meaning for Donna, myself and others in these early years of the 21st century. I understand the Incarnation as the interface between divinity and creation, spirit and matter, humanity and the other-than-human world – the birth of a child, the unfolding of a flower, and the birth of an insight, project or community like ours around the holiday table.

On this Christmas day in New Jersey as the rain turns to snow, the meal is complete. In the companionable silence that follows, I hear whispers about the birth of newness. Once again incarnation happens, divinity is present, and the earth community vibrates with new life.

Donna gathers her presents of clothes, candy and cards, and with happy smiles takes her leave to be driven home by Fran. As they vanish into the night, I am conscious of my own wounds and weaknesses, sometimes more hidden than our guest's. The meaning of Christmas seems clearer now. Divinity has visited us in the person of a woman, Donna, whose very wounds and uncomplicated wisdom were the manger of newness on this Incarnation Day.

Bethlehem Needs to Happen

Bethlehem needs to happen:

Through the welcoming of world religions into a unity of planetary peace.

In the celebration of science, art and mysticism, to recover a new origin story for our lives.

Through radical listening and storytelling, so that we may come home to the rich soil of our psyches.

That we may recover the wisdom of a theology of the Incarnation and may find in the "differentiated unity" of the Trinity, a basis for reverence and love.

That we may find, in the liberating practices of cultural work, primary actions for freedom and geo-justice making.

In places of worship, so that healing can come to our bodies, to our imaginations, and to our authentic desire to create, through the arts and the art of prayer, the art of our lives.

In hospital emergency rooms and outpatient clinics, so welcoming can happen and compassion can be born.

In school classrooms so that feelings, intuitions and ideas can commune and holistic learning can take place.

So that capitalism can be healed of its competition and social policy can recover a sensitivity to spirit.

So that acquisitiveness and lifestyles of apparent necessity can give way to simplicity and a reverential use of energy.

So that gatherings and communities can respect differences, while individuals and outsiders can be welcomed into fabrics of support and solution.

So that spring can continually be born of winter, that the seasons of the earth can also be the seasons of our heart.

That we may reverence creation for its own sake and in fields of plenty grow bread for a hungry world.

In libraries, in institutes for cancer and AIDS research, in detox centres, and places of hospitality for the poor and lonely.

Where waters are poisoned, the earth is pummelled with fertilizers, and the air is rancid with acid rain.

When the aspirations of youth are crushed by cynicism and the wisdom of age is discarded and repressed.

So that we can see in the Incarnation of Christmas — an event that continues today, a genesis that continues to happen in our cosmos, in our psyches, and in our souls — an incarnation story of our time, a story emerging from the heart of oneness.

Reflections at the Edge of Soul

*You have to have a definition of self that's grounded
in how connected we all are to each other.*

—Mary Ford

The spiritual journey contains a variety of ingredients: courage, openness, compassion, integral consciousness and love, which is the expression of a generous and abundant universe.

Through mystical engagement we contemplate the depths of the psyche and receive images, symbols and archetypes from the wellspring of our soul.

As we bring to conscious expression what lies in the recesses of our psyches, we fashion a holistic spirituality that is aligned to the cosmos, resides within the soul, and culminates in a compassionate commitment to the prophetic struggle.

> *Without mysticism politics soon becomes cruel and barbaric; without political love mysticism becomes sentimental or uncommitted interiority.*
>
> —Edward Schillebeeckx

A Deeper Life

Mary Oliver's poem "The Journey" explores the dream from a mythological and cosmological perspective. The question is, "Where is my place in the universe? What am I here for? And what are the indicators that will help me understand and feel at peace?" Thomas Merton said, "If I never become the person I'm supposed to be, I'm going to spend the rest of my life contradicting myself." Many of us spend our lives in a state of unclarity. Achieving clarity doesn't involve manipulating the universe to our own ends. It's a process of discovery that continues to unfold.

The Journey

One day you finally knew
what you had to do, and began,
though the voices around you
kept shouting
their bad advice —
though the whole house
began to tremble
and you felt the old tug
at your ankles.
"Mend my life!"
each voice cried.
But you didn't stop.
You knew what you had to do,
though the wind pried
with its stiff fingers
at the very foundations,
though their melancholy
was terrible.

It was already late
enough, and a wild night,
and the road full of fallen
branches and stones.
But little by little,
as you left their voices behind,
the stars began to burn
through the sheets of clouds,
and there was a new voice
which you slowly
recognized as your own
that kept you company
as you strode deeper and deeper
into the world,
determined to do
the only thing you could do – determined to save
the only life you could save.

—Mary Oliver

As Mary Oliver reminds us, the challenge is to take our life in our own hands. When we do, we have a greater capacity to fulfill our life purpose. The poem reminds us not to listen to bad advice, but to listen to the inner voice for the invitation, the vocation, the calling. Parker Palmer writes, "Vocation does not come from wilfulness. It comes from listening.... It means a call that I hear." A vocation is a calling, a voice from outside that summons us.

When our calling comes, we might be asked to take our life into our own hands just when things seem least clear to us. Pain and loss often open the door to our true self. Ernesto Cardinale, the great Nicaraguan poet, says that when we hear the call, we will be prompted by our discontent. Something in us will tell us that we've been off course. When we become physically ill, we know there's something wrong. The same thing is true of our life's direction. If we're troubled in our hearts, then something is off course.

Often the very significant things that change our life seem insignificant at the moment they happen; when we look back later we recognize them as turning points. It could have been a phone call, a gesture, an insight, a trip – a moment when we took a new direction, when we knew what we had to do, and began.

The voice of vocation doesn't lead us to exactly where our heroes have been. We're not here to be another Gandhi, or King, or Teresa of Avila, or Mother Teresa. Though we might be inspired by such people, inspiration is not authentic if it leads only to a rigid imitation. The challenge is not to repeat their lives but to learn how they brought them about – how they changed the culture to make their vision a possibility. That's the imitation that our ancestors are calling us to.

How can we be true to ourselves? Mary Oliver says that we are here "to save the only life that we can save." To me that means being true to our inner wisdom, promptings, indicators – the moments of synchronicity and those sacred impulses that guide us toward the future. Most of us have tapes inside of us – the voices of our parents, of institutions, of authority figures – that have conditioned us to respond in ways that are less than authentic. What is authentic is often what we know for certain without being able to explain why. From that knowing we stride deeper and deeper into the world. "To save the only life that you can save" is to answer your calling.

Vocation in our world is usually associated with a job. We define ourselves by our functions, our professions. But we are not what we do for a living. One of the ways to ask ourselves what we're called to is to see what we are preoccupied with, what we are passionate about, what we are competent in. What are our gifts? What are we committed to? The call to a deeper life is not about the external lifestyle choices we have made. It's not about our religious life or whether we're married or single. It's about the call within the call, about what summons each of us to be our authentic self.

Unfortunately, many of the contexts available for us do not support the inner promptings. We have to change society so that we can have a context for our calling. As we change paradigms and cosmologies, we also change the context in which we live our lives. Our lives must be culturally connected to the unfolding of the universe.

It's been more than a decade since Nelson Mandela was released from prison. Here's a man whose inspiration has permeated the whole culture. He didn't become bitter during his years of imprisonment. He stayed a prophet in the cell block. We too are in the cell blocks of our own culture. We're all doing time. We're incarcerated in the oppressive structures of our society. We can learn from Nelson Mandela to emancipate ourselves and the oppressive forces around us. This is our task, our call to deeper life.

Growing Our Soul

An integral spirituality identifies and responds to issues that impact the planet and our lives; it evokes imagination and courage; it is written in the narrative of people's lives and inscribed in the story of the universe. It is nurtured by passion, moral outrage and hope; it is discovered and expressed through trust, listening and soul work; it finds expression in a new-found freedom for people and the planet.

When I was a young boy growing up in Ontario, Canada, I lived on the baseball diamond. My brother and I would often go out to visit the man who was our coach and talk with him about life. One day I arrived to find his wife, Dorothy, walking around in the backyard, under the apple trees. I asked her what she was doing, and she said, "I'm just out here in the backyard growin' my soul." My question for us is, how do we grow our soul? What was Dorothy talking about, and what can we learn from her?

There are ten spiritual practices I'd like to highlight that contribute to our journey into sacredness and depth. They are listening, heeding the prophets, letting go, remembering, exercising compassion, celebrating creativity, spending time with the little ones, honouring the beauty of creation, making authentic rituals, and harbouring hope and vision.

Listening

Listening is the capacity not just to hear with our ears, but to be open to whatever and wherever the universe chooses to communicate with us – from a bird, a breeze, a tree, or in the prophetic voice of a Martin Luther King, Jr. or a Mahatma Gandhi, or in the canonical texts of our traditions, whether the Hebrew or Christian Bible, the Koran, or the ancestral voices. Such a listening heart also enables us to attend to the promptings of our own souls. In my book *Sacred Impulse*, I propose that intuition, the capacity to be open to what some would call "that still small voice" – the divine nudge, the visceral response – is an expression of such listening.

Part of listening is giving recognition to another. Listening is not about giving advice. When someone talks about her life, you don't need to have answers for her. She isn't really looking for them from you. She just wants someone to listen. Most of us have our own answers; we long for an opportunity to access the clarity that exists deep within us. That clarity comes through being listened to, and being able to listen to ourselves. Recognition provides the attention that makes the listening possible. It's both a great challenge and also a priceless gift just to listen.

One definition for spirituality is that it's the capacity for a listening heart. The listening heart is sensitive and receptive to all of the interactions and relationships that we both endure and celebrate. We listen with the ears of the soul. Listening and recognition are at the centre of the spiritual life and are a profound way to grow our soul. Brother David Steindl-Rast, OSB, says that a listening heart involves the experience of faith, hope and love through existential trust, openness to surprise and saying "yes" to belonging.

Heeding the Prophets

Another way to grow our soul is to listen to and to be inspired by the voices of the prophets. The late Dom Hêlder Câmara, the Bishop of Recife in Brazil, who was one of the great voices of the poor in the church after Vatican II, wrote, "Anytime, day or night, at home or in the street, wherever we are, we live bathed in God." That is the voice of a prophet.

It is important to understand that neither the prophets of the Old Testament, Daniel and Samuel and Isaiah, nor the prophets or our time, such as King, Gandhi, Dorothy Day, Cesar Chavez, Bede Griffith, Thomas Merton, and perhaps your own ancestors, are asking us to imitate them. They are asking us to be inspired by our own vision, energized by their words so we can find our own way, our own response to this prophetic moment – in the church, in the workplace, in the family, and in the society that truly needs our help. Rabbi Heschel, the great Jewish mystic, wrote, "There's a grain of the prophet in the recesses of every human soul." It is such a vision that calls upon us to be a people of protest and prophecy, to stand on our principles, to speak truth to power, and to dare to tell the truth.

Today, prophets are being recognized as they confront the issue of globalization. We hear accounts from Seattle, Prague, Washington, Québec City, and Detroit which point up two worldwide trends. The first is the globalization of the corporate "free market" that is really separating the rich and the poor, that is invading people with its extractive economy, moving into countries, paying sweatshop wages and then taking the products back to another land to be sold at a great profit. That's the globalization that prophetic people are protesting.

The second trend is toward another kind of globalization which is wonderful and needs to be expanded. It's the globalization of the human rights movements and what I think of as the "second superpower," the emerging movement for planetary peace. It's the globalization of the ecological and environmental movements that are converging in South America, in Central America and in this country as well. Our prophetic voices need to stand on the side of the planet and the people who cry out for a new world community.

I envision a council of all beings, where humans stand in the centre and all the other species have a chance to talk to the humans about how they have mistreated the land: "I don't like what you're doing to my water," or, "Why did you cut down my trees?" Then the humans come to the outside and apologize to all the other species who are now in the centre. A Council of All Species would be a kind of "ecozoic council," to use Thomas Berry's phrase. It would support and energize the prophetic groups that are springing up all over the country and all over the world. We need to lend our voices to making the planet a mutually enriching place to live, not just for us, but for the children of the next generation and beyond.

Letting Go

Almost every tradition has a dimension of letting go, even if it uses different language to describe it. Buddhism talks about the dangers of attachment, which could also be described as clinging. It's the clinging, not the object of the attachment, that is the problem. One of the reasons that we have a pathological culture is our collective inability to let go.

Culture is made up of many elements that differ from people to people: different stories, different music, different ancestral myths, different creation stories, different art forms, different rituals, different values, different media, ethics and customs. Our spirituality is intimately connected to all these cultural elements. It's embodied. It's contextualized. If we judge some element of our culture to be pathological, we need to seek a spiritual practice which will allow us to engage in cultural therapy to heal the illness we experience. One such practice is the process of letting go.

In the life of the medieval mystic John of the Cross we find a powerful example of the practice of letting go. He suffered abuse, pain and incarceration, but he did not hold on to anger, bitterness or despair. John of the Cross wrote about what he called "the dark night of the soul." Some would describe the dark night as the experience of falling out of a plane and feeling your parachute won't open. We're living today in the dark night of our cultural soul as well as of our personal experiences. We need to learn to break through our fear, let go of the unnecessary limitations we place on our envisioning of what life can be.

Two examples of such breakthrough experiences in our lives are to fall in love or to have a nervous breakdown. Both imply an absence of defences and an energy that wants to be released. In the latter case our culture pathologizes this energy: drugs it, shocks it and closes it down. Falling in love, which is more socially acceptable, is having such an affinity for someone, some idea or some passion, that the obstacles to intimacy are dissolved. Love gives us the opportunity to get out of the way, to let go of whatever holds us back. Classical psychotherapy would call this "ego death." Teilhard describes this as shattering our mental categories, transforming how we see the world internally. Dom Hêlder Câmara shows us another route to such a breakthrough when he counsels: "Allow things to happen; accept surprises that upset your plans." In other words, let go. The process of letting go is catalyzed by events in our lives. It is a spiritual strategy for dealing with pain, disappointment, and all of the bitter and burdensome events that are part and parcel of our lives.

The opposite of letting go is thinking that we have all the answers, that we have a predetermined plan for our lives, that we've got it all figured out ahead of time. Letting go means that the creative energy of the divine is allowed expression within and through us. It's like being on a sailboat when the wind comes up and allowing it to take the boat on a new course. That wind takes us to a place we could never have discovered on our own. When our mental categories shatter in such a way, we can feel the turbulence inside; the way we saw the world is challenged and reorganized.

Another dimension of the letting go process is coming to terms with the fact that we are divine but not God. Divinization is not equivalent to being God. Letting go means moving from narcissism to mysticism. Narcissism is when we're centred on ourselves in our inordinate psychic introspection. Everything is us. The world circles around us. Mysticism is cosmic-centred: it is a oneness with all that is. Gratitude means we let go of the sense that we have an inherent right to be and begin to see life as a gift. This is a major and necessary shift if we are to grow spiritually.

We also have to let go of the belief that we are unhealable. One reason there is so much therapy is that we don't believe it works. Woody Allen's joke about therapy is "One more session and I'm going to Lourdes." We often use therapy to convince ourselves that only a miracle could cure us. This flows from the misguided conception implied in the idea of original sin that we are unhealable. Part of the process of letting go is forgiving ourselves, acknowledging our original goodness and realizing that we are still inherently good. Letting go is also about forgiving others. Forgiving those who have offended us is letting go of the enemy.

And what about letting go of a dull life or one lived only in memory? Norman Cousins says, "The tragedy of life is not death, but what we let die inside while we are still alive." I had a friend who was a hospice nurse and was at our program in Oakland a few years ago. When she talked to her patients, many of whom had cancer, she would ask them: "How has cancer blessed your life?" The stories of gratitude that she heard were amazing. On some deep level, we know that whatever happens, it redounds to good. Think of your own stories of grief and loss and letting go, whether it's a spouse, a relationship, an occupation or an illness. At one moment, it feels devastating, and it is, but ultimately something new shines through those moments. It's part of the human journey, the act of surrender and letting go. Meister Eckhart says it this way: "God is not found in the soul by adding anything, but by a process of subtraction."

When I was a little boy in Ontario, we had a pear tree in the backyard. My father would prune it, and after he cut some of the branches off, the poor thing looked rather withered and unspectacular. But then the next year, guess what? Bigger pears! Juicier pears. We grow our soul just like that pear tree. When things somehow are, or appear to be, taken from us, it creates the opportunity for something new to come through. It's a great paradox, but it's profound and always present. The soul grows by subtraction. That's worth meditating on.

If I never become what I am meant to be, but always remain what I am not,
I shall spend eternity contradicting myself by being at once something
and nothing,
a life that wants to live and is dead
and a death that wants to be dead
and cannot quite achieve its own death because it still has to exist.
—Thomas Merton

Detachment is more important than love.
—Meister Eckhart

Remembering

Storytelling is at the centre of the spiritual journey. Remembering is about story-ing. Jack Shea is a great storyteller. He wrote *Stories of God, Stories of Faith,* and *Gospel Light.* He says if you feel consoled, inspired and healed by stories, it's because they've connected you with the loving vitality of soul. Therefore one way to grow your soul is to tell your story. Reflect on your story. When you gather with groups, in "wisdom circles," tell your stories – the stories of your ancestors, the stories of your grandkids, or your children, or your communities, the stories of your tradition, the stories of the universe – the stories of all those things that you hold dear.

Stories are the way we connect with each other. Every tradition uses stories as a vehicle for communication. We tell stories as a way of identifying who we are. Our culture also has stories as does our universe. Our lives can be viewed from these three perspectives: the personal, the cultural and the cosmic. The stories we're writing about ourselves, and the story of society, and the story of the universe are all one story. One of the major insights of our time is that our lives are chapters in the big story.

When you get to know somebody you want to hear their story. You want to know where that person came from, what their origins are, where they've been. From that you might have some idea where they are at this moment and who they are. We discover our own identity through storytelling. Classic psychotherapy is storytelling. Therapy is changing our personal story, from woundology to original goodness. That's the process of healing. In cosmology, we locate our story within the larger universe. A story energizes us. There's something about being able to tell our story that heals us, that makes pain more bearable.

The spiritual practice of storytelling is the practice of remembering. You can't tell a story without a memory. Stories reveal changes and transformational moments. The shifts that happen over time are incorporated into our stories. Self-reflective consciousness is the unique gift of humanity. We are the universe reflecting on itself. When we tell our stories, we are also speaking on behalf of the Earth.

Richard Harmon of the Industrial Areas Foundation NW Regional Office in Portland, Oregon says, "When we speak from the center of our sacredness, the Earth in its pain and tenderness is speaking through us." Stories are a way that we achieve meaning. Patricia Mische, Co-founder of Global Education Associates and Professor of Peace Studies, says, "Stories are like membranes – they connect the world of our lives to the world out there." They're semi-permeable membranes. Helen Prejean, author of *Dead Man Walking*, says, "There's no truth, only stories." When we tell stories and see the universe as a story, we're remembering the series of transformational events that appear over time, out of which this present moment evolves.

When we tell someone our story, we speak of defining moments. Thomas Berry would call them "moments of grace," those gifts of opportunity when transformation is possible. Story is a way to access and express those moments of transformation. A story also knits together our inner fragmentation and then connects us to others so that we don't feel alone.

Our story is a dimension of the universe story. The story of the universe can be understood in four chapters: the galactic period from the flaring forth and formation of the elements; the formation of the Earth itself; the beginning-of-life period, when plants and animals emerge; and our chapter, the human period, marked by the rise of culture and consciousness. Though in our culture we tend to think of story as something written down in a book, something communicated exclusively with words, the stories we're talking about are broader than that. The birds tell the story, the sun tells the story, the music, the breeze. Stories are communicated on many levels – sound and smell and image and light and darkness. Thomas Berry, the great geologian, cultural historian and Passionist priest, says we explain things by telling their story: how they came into being and the changes that have taken place over time. Each person is a story unfolding in time, and so is the universe whose story, and therefore ours, began unfolding about thirteen billion years ago.

Every story is revelation. The divine is communicated to us through story. Our culture tends to have a narrow vision of revelation, to confine it to the canonical scriptures and the time before the death of the last apostle – revelation is boxed in. In the cosmological view, revelation happens daily, moment by moment. It's happening right now. It's always unfolding. Implications of that story are that everything is valuable, that all dimensions of life should be represented in any decision-making process, that the divine is present everywhere, that diversity is something to celebrate and not repress.

The New Story is not just a poetic good-hearted way of seeing the world, but the basic truth.

—Elizabeth Johnson

Practising Compassion

Compassion is being in an equal relationship with those in need, whether human or other-than-human. Compassion is not doing something for someone to make them feel inferior. Meister Eckhart says, "The soul is where God works compassion." We grow our soul by the practice of compassion.

Eckhart also says the best name for God is Compassion. My image of compassion is that of a mother embracing her child, holding her close while being willing to let go when the time comes. This reminds me of the divine embrace of the universe, which I see as a curvature of compassion. We live in the arms of a universe where there's a balance between the forces of expansion and gravity. If either element were out of balance, our universe would not exist. The point of harmony is an expression of the curvature of compassion. This key reality of our universe, that our life depends on achieving equilibrium, is reflected in many aspects of human life such as our striving to balance our need for both continuity and discontinuity, or innovation and tradition, in healthy ways. We need continuity with our roots, but we also need to live in this moment, making the tradition present and palpable today. Reflecting on the image of the divine curvature of compassion will give us insight, strength and compassion as we work to change the structures and world view that have become desacralized.

The practice of compassion is always to be in relationship with the *anawim*, those "little ones without a voice." All of us feel at times like we are members of the anawim in our churches and in our society. It's through finding the compassionate curve that results from embracing each other while mining the gold underneath the crust of our traditions that will nurture our lives. Imagine a volcano like the ones in Hawaii. When it is erupting, everything's fluid and warm and moving. After a while, however, the flow turns to rock, becomes rigid and stuck. We need theological air hammers to release the molten places underneath that crust of tradition so as to uncover the prophetic voice where there's still that fluid, that passionate voice of compassion that is reaching out to the little ones. Juan Sobrino, a Jesuit priest from El Salvador who narrowly escaped assassination, says, "The poor transmit realities and values which are very difficult to find outside their world." In hope, commitment, community, celebration, creativity, transcendence and compassion we experience the life of our tradition.

Celebrating Creativity

The imagination is at the heart of being fully human. Eckhart says, "If your heart is troubled, you're not yet a mother, you're still on the way to giving birth." What he meant by that is that there's a sense of dis-ease if we're not being creative, a feeling that something isn't right with us. Creativity is not dualistic. It's not objectifying: it is a mystical experience of being one with the clay, the painting or the dance. There's an art gallery in Kleinburg, just north of Toronto, that houses the work of the Group of Seven. One of these Canadian artists, Lawren Harris, has painted wonderful sunsets and sunrises. Somebody asked him one time, "Lawren, what does it mean for you to be creative?" and he said, "When I paint, I try to get to the summit of my soul, and I paint from there, where the universe sings."

Creativity is at the heart of us. When we talk about "soul music" and "soul food," it's all about the heart. Creativity is giving expression to what lies deep within our hearts. You can do that in a conversation with your spouse. You can do that in your work, with your children, with your colleagues, in your community. Creativity is not limited to a paintbrush, or to a studio. It enlivens the studio of our lives where we create and re-create life itself. We are never more like God than when we are creating. Each individual is unique, a reflection of the divine, and our acts of creation enhance the likeness. Freud said of his work, "Everywhere I go I find a poet has been there before me." A scientist I know in British Columbia was working on a complicated theorem. One creative person took a look at the problem and gave him the answer. It was ten years before they worked out the equations. The artist always leads. The imagination precedes the intellect, always. Using our imaginations, allowing our creative hearts to express themselves in all areas of our lives, grows our souls.

Relating to the Little Ones

Meister Eckhart wrote, "If I was really frightened, I would like to have a child with me, and if there were no children around, I would like an animal." This quote always reminds me of Mark, a wonderful young man I met a few years ago who seemed to radiate goodness. His mother told me that when he was applying to the university for admission to a graduate program, he wrote the mandatory essay, which was a major part of determining whether or not he'd be accepted, about his dog, Maxie. The essay could have been a daunting task but Mark took his dog with him into it and did just fine. His story suggests to me what Eckhart was telling us, that being close to a little one, whether a child or an animal, is a way of accessing our connection to God. It's a way to deal with our fears. It's a way to grow our soul. Gustavo Gutierrez writes, "God is more present in the little ones." Somehow the image of the divine is often revealed to us more clearly through the unprotected and the un-powerful.

Honouring the Beauty of Creation

To experience the beauty of creation is to have a sacramental consciousness by which we recognize the face of God in all of nature. This is another kind of literacy that all of us are capable of, but sometimes not conscious of, when we read God's face in a sunrise or sunset, a bluebonnet flower, a storm, a mountain range, a prairie, an ocean. These are the moments when creation speaks to us and tells us the story of the universe. David Steindl-Rast, the great Benedictine of our time, says, "When we experience creation through the senses, we experience God." And St. Bernard wrote: "You will learn more in the woods than you will in books. The trees and the stones will teach you what you will never learn in the school of the masters." Jim Couture, a graduate of the Sophia Center program, wrote: "The cavity of our souls needs to be filled with the wonder and awe of the natural world." We grow our soul every time we respond to such beauty.

Making Authentic Rituals

Ritual is the language of the soul. Why do we have ritual? Because we need symbolic language to express the deeper recesses of our hearts and minds and souls, to connect the conscious to the unconscious. There are "cultural rituals" inspired by a spiritual impulse such as the gatherings around Ground Zero, the testimonies at Oklahoma City, the processions for peace, or outside an institution that is about to practise the death penalty. Rabbi Heschel says, "Prayers are meaningless unless they are subversive."

Eucharists don't all happen in churches. One Holy Thursday, I was privileged to be with a group of people in San Francisco in what is called the Tenderloin (the inner city). Mary Ann Finch works with a group called Care Through Touch Institute. We were celebrating Holy Thursday by practising the gospel mandate of Jesus to wash the feet of the poor as an act of service and generosity and inclusion. We went around in groups and massaged the feet of the homeless as a gesture of service. It was incredibly joyful. Touching these people's feet often turned on 50 years of story. It just poured out of them.

One woman said, "I wrote to all my grandchildren." Her marriage was broken and she hadn't seen her family for years. She had written to all her granddaughters back in Massachusetts; only one of them answered her. Just one of them. She went upstairs to the little room she lives in and brought down the letter to show me. It said, "Dear Grandma, I have your picture on my desk and when I do my homework, I look at you and I love you." That meant a lot to that woman. Even though her other grandchildren didn't answer, she was joyful because one of them did. In this ritual we both grew souls and, I believe, that act of service was Eucharist; together we re-enacted the Last Supper. Communion was happening. As Miriam Therese Winter says, "There's little-e Eucharist and there's big-E Eucharist. Little-e Eucharist happens when we communicate, not necessarily only when we commune." And it happens a lot.

Prayer is the movement from illusion to reality. It's less about changing God's mind than about embracing the reality of our own lives.

Envisioning

To grow our soul we need to have hope, a vision and a dream of what our life could be. There's nothing sadder than a life spent just going through the motions. John O'Donohue says, "The greatest tragedy is the unlived life." A lot of people are going through the motions, just hanging in there, always waiting, never taking the initiative. For them, life has no deep meaning. We all need a vision and a dream to keep hope alive and to lead us to ask and seek an answer for Mary Oliver's question: "What is it you plan to do with your one wild and precious life?"

It takes a vision and a dream to draw you forward, to help you attend to that still small voice within, to the synchronicities of events; to discern your truth in what you hear from the pulpit, from your colleagues, from your spouse, from your children, from your puppy. At some moment the shape of your future will become clearer and you will identify and claim the visions that were yours when you were born. Yours will not be an unlived life.

We can also grow our soul to recognize and respect the sacredness and depth in what might seem to be unlikely places. A group called the Community Action Network in Dublin works with people who are homeless, who suffer from domestic violence, addiction or unemployment, and other forms of human pathos that are so prevalent. When they get together they ask people to go out and walk in the streets of the city. They have one requirement – that you walk with your "soul eyes" open. "Soul eyes" allow a person to see the sacredness and depth in all they encounter on their walk.

When the members of this group return, they report seeing syringes on the street, a flower bursting forth in a garden, a homeless person, a child, the rain – everything with new compassion and clarity.

Soul Work/Prayer/Spiritual Practice

Soul work moves us from illusion to reality; it is less about petition and contrition than attuning our lives and minds to the unfolding dynamics of the universe.

Soul work is an encounter with beauty and pain, an expression of gratitude and a search for meaning, a language that transcends all traditions.

In spiritual practice we become a poet and a politician.

In soul work we contact the pulsating, originating energy of the universe; through receptivity and response we experience what we long for and dive deeply into the joys and sorrows of life and experience the solidarity of engagement.

Soul work and spiritual practice are an attitude of the heart, an openness to the meaning of existence. Through soul work we gain perspective on God's action in the world.

In our spiritual practice we realize that challenge, fear, gratitude, hope for possibilities and tendencies towards self-destruction are present in all people. We discover that life's mysteries are present in everyone. Our spiritual practice emerges from our deepest intuitions and is understood as universal for everyone.

Sound spiritual practice is dialectical (e.g., progressive and conservative, innovative and traditional).

Soul work names and celebrates the dramatic moments of creativity and new life; we name the human journey within the context of the paschal mystery, and intensify the mystery and name in everyday existence. We become continuously reminded that tomorrow can be different than today, that our deepest longings have a cosmic and sacred source.

Prayer happens through our interaction with others; it is here we discover who we are. It is here that revelation happens. Through our engagements we choose again and again the path to transformation and discover that life on earth is possible.

Soul work happens in stillness. In transparent moments we perceive the universe. We experience gratitude and joy, validity and purpose, and become energized for the journey toward meaning and fulfillment.

In our soul work we enhance our visual literacy and discover a language of the soul, a language that speaks of "popular piety," "veranda narratives" and vocational destiny.

Our soul work includes silent recollection and engaged action, a vulnerability to wonder, an invitation to mystery, an openness to reverence, an experience of belonging, and an awareness of the sacredness of life.

Soul work provides access to identity and reveals our place in the community of life.

Our spiritual practice involves dialogue, listening, communal ritual and critical reflection. Spiritual practice activates a radical response to life, and a moral embrace of the Commandments of Creation:

- Celebrate difference and honour creativity.
- Nurture communion and express compassion.
- Revere depth and the soul of all sentient beings.

And now I think for the first time in my whole life, I really began to pray...praying not with my lips and with my intellect and my imagination but praying out of the very roots of my life and of my being and praying to the God I had never known.

—Thomas Merton

Praying is nothing but the inhaling and exhaling of one breath of the universe.

—Hildegard of Bingen

Prayer ones the soul to God.

—Julian of Norwich

Our spirituality is earth-derived...the thoughts and emotions, the social forms and rituals of the human community, are as much "earth" as is the soil and the rocks and trees and flowers.

—Thomas Berry

Personal saviour orientation has led to an interpersonal devastationalism that quite easily dispenses with earth except as a convenient support for life.

—Thomas Berry

Any religion that professes to be concerned with the souls of a people and is not concerned with the slums that damn them, the economic conditions that strangle them and the social conditions that cripple them is a dry-as-dust religion.

—Martin Luther King, Jr.

Justice is just another name for God. Every living and non-living event is sacred. Every creature is sacred. Every person is sacred. Our vocation is to help draw out the image of God within the members of our species.

—Abraham Heschel

The scientific story of creation is magnificent and enormous and provides a context for all religions to articulate their experience of the sacred.

—Richard Harmon

Let your universal presence spring forth in a blaze that is at once diaphany and fire.

—Teilhard de Chardin

Despite frequent comments about secularization in Western society...interest in spirituality is certainly not confined to churchgoers or those commonly identified as religious people.

—Philip Sheldrake

The poet needs the practicalities of making a living to test and temper the lyricism of insight and observation. The composition needs the poet's insight and powers of attention in order to weave the inner world of soul creativity with the outer world of form and matter.

—David Whyte

A new day is dawning on our spiritual landscape and new possibilities for spiritual pilgrimage open up on all sides.

—Diarmuid O'Murchu

Equilibrium...
Favoured words of mystics...
A high wire act, one foot firm
One in mid air.

—Daniel Berrigan

The most important spiritual question of our time is also the most
important spiritual question of any time: how does one live in
communion with God, under whatever name – the Holy, the Sacred,
the Transcendent, the Wholly Other, Being?

—Richard McBrien

A richly elaborated life connected to society and nature, woven into
the culture of family, nature, and globe.

—Thomas Moore

If the ultimate aim of prayer is to deepen our faith and nurture a
healthy spirituality, the test of all prayer will not be how intense and
uplifting it was or what insights we had. It will be the extent to which
it leads us to allow the spirit of graciousness and generosity to be
evident in the way we are neighbours to one another.

How willing are we to let ourselves be freely led by the presence and
power within us?

—Michael Morwood

Each of us must take our place in the unfolding mystery that is at the
heart of the universe.

—Miriam MacGillis

The New Story becomes the wineskin for every story ever told.

—Carmel Higgins

To pray is an act of courage; it presumes greatness and expansiveness
of spirit and heart beyond the boundless time and open space of the
vast cosmos.

—Leonardo Boff

Primarily we are experiencing sentiments of awe and wonder arising from the inner depths of the soul. Prayer is a disposition that exposes the soul to relational energy.

—Diarmuid O'Murchu

Prayer is an encounter with the more.

—Br. David Steindl-Rast, OSB

Prayer is the highest achievement of which the human person is capable.

—Edith Stein

Prayer is the movement of the Holy Spirit in the human heart through which God reaches out and embraces human beings.

—Glenstal Book of Prayer

Prayer can be understood as the last moment of speech before the silence.

—Karl Rahner

He also speaks through life...that new gospel to which we add a page each day.

—Michael Quoist

These life moments (Gratitude, Letting go, Waiting, Creativity and Action) are the context of prayer. They invite us to get in touch with the source and center of life, whom we call God.

—Alexandra Kovats

Instead of the prayer of petition...the prayer of praise and thanks to God and the prayer of lamentation characterize the companionship model.

Our prayers and action are conscientiously directed to bringing about the coming of the kingdom of God.

—Teilhard de Chardin

At This Moment

At this moment
I straddle the intersections of life

And choose at this crossroad of existence
To endure the pain of dislocation
And be freed from the conformity of trodden paths

May the guiding star of a tomorrow
Promise to illuminate the sky
Access the wisdom of a child
Now healed from denial and despair
To once again relentlessly pursue
A Deeper purpose and avoid an as yet unlived life.

Artists of Life

The most visible creators I know are those artists whose medium is life
itself. The ones who express the inexpressible without brush, hammer,
clay, or guitar.
They neither paint nor sculpt. Their medium is being.
Whatever their presence touches has increased life.
They see and don't have to draw.
They are the artists of being alive.

—Anonymous

When cosmologist Brian Swimme was writing *The Hidden Heart of the Cosmos,* his working title was *The All-Nourishing Abyss.* He meant that nothingness is the source of life, ideas, universe and creativity. The original fireball – that creative moment that marks the beginning of the universe – cannot be calculated from the very beginning point. There is a time, a mysterious moment, which people of faith would call the divine creative act. Out of nothingness, in a sense, everything is born. It's my conviction that the most profound impulse, the most sacred longing of soul that any of us has, is to understand and express our creativity.

Creativity is the impulse inside us that has to find expression. It will do so either in a benevolent way or in a destructive way. Much of the violence in our culture is repressed creativity, as is much of the burnout in our workaday world. Institutional structures are afraid of change and therefore do not encourage creativity.

Creativity, however, is not just one option among many. It's a precondition for an authentic life. Many people spend the first half of their lives *doing* things and then the second half of their lives *discovering who they are*. The problem with such self-discovery occurs when we rely on psychological technologies to tell us who we are. "I'm a 6." "I'm an INFP." "I'm an obsessive-compulsive." I don't think that psychological techniques reveal the authentic self. I'm not saying that enneagrams and Myers-Briggs and other psychological tools aren't valid but that they don't really get to the core of who we are. The way we discover ourselves is through the creative act, not through psychological technology.

Creativity takes courage. Anastasia MacDonald, a Sophia Center graduate and my work-study student while I was preparing a manuscript, coined a word: *creageous*. She combined *courage* and *creativity* into one word. The prophets of today are people of courage and creativity. They are the saints of tomorrow, and are often exiled in their own time. Anastasia wrote a poem expanding on the word's definition:

> Deciding without knowing where it will take me,
> Returning to my easel when the paints made me cry last week,
> Dancing no matter who is watching,
> Writing when there is no language to express my experience,
> Being silent and listening,
> Pursuing subjects that make me nervous,
> Singing to hear my voice,
> Raising my hand and saying "I will,"
> Asking for dreams night after night,
> Creageous is stepping off looking up not down.

Creativity and the Prophetic Voice

> Art is the vehicle for mystery.
>
> —Robert Lenz

Prophetic voices are often exiled in the times in which they live and then canonized in the years that follow. Look at Teilhard de Chardin for example. For the last ten years of his life he was permitted to publish only manuscripts that were exclusively scientific.

Fortunately he had trusted friends, so, soon after his death, *The Phenomenon of Man* and *The Divine Milieu* became best-sellers! At any conference in the post–Vatican II church these books could be seen tucked under people's arms. Teilhard's writings are the foundation stone of our current cosmological work. In his time and church, however, evolution was seen as suspect. Today, evolution is generally acknowledged to be a viable hypothesis.

The Creative Process

The creative process is the closest we get to the divine. It is the doorway into the New Story. One can't be a machine, or think like one, and be creative. The two are incompatible. The creative process is about unleashing the imagination and entering into the spirit of mysticism, which can be understood as the resurrection of our soul. It is the consciousness of a new world view. In our deepest self we are at one with the universe, with ourselves, with one another, with Creation and with the divine. Standing on the corner of 4th and Walnut in downtown Louisville, Thomas Merton suddenly said, "I love everybody! I am awakening from the dream of separateness." *That's* what creativity does for us. It awakens us from the dream of separateness – from the nightmare of urban blight, the despair of the youth, the old people who are being put into filing cabinets called retirement communities, the distance and alienation from the very source of our own life and being.

One of the first steps to the creative process is learning to be silent. Learning to live with silence. Rilke says, "Is there enough silence, so I can hear?" We say at the Sophia Center that wisdom is the capacity for a listening heart. Through a *listening* heart we are tuned in, and attuned, to the voice within and the voice without. Stories are based on listening and recognition. There is no story if nobody listens. There is no story if there is no one to tell it. Silence is the birthplace of creativity. It also gives us the capacity to move beyond illusion to reality. The media, on the other hand, can be a vehicle for illusion, for propaganda, or, as Noam Chomsky would put it, "manufactured consent." The creative process requires a movement from illusion to reality. What blocks us are our misconceptions about who we are or what it is we are called to create.

Spiritual practices, such as meditation, ritual, movement, journalling and conversations with a friend, are a precondition for creativity. All of these deepen the process and unleash the imagination. Sabbatical time, whether a year away to study, a couple of hours in the park, or time for a walk with a child, friend or puppy, is also necessary. At its deepest level, it reminds us that the world will survive without us. Things will go on. Sabbatical time means being able to live without *doing* something. It means rest, leisure, a time to catch our breath. Often our best ideas occur when we're not trying to solve a problem. When we want to grind away at an idea but instead go for a walk, all of a sudden the very things we were trying to deal with fall into place. Sabbatical time is a source of the creative process.

There are many people who have put words to this process. Gregory Baum lives in Montreal and is Professor Emeritus at McGill University. He says, "Creativity is what we believe in." In other words, faith is in the imagination. What we really believe in is what we create. Not what we *claim* we believe in, but what we actually create, reveals our deepest conviction. This is worth thinking about because often our traditions are reduced to tenets of belief rather than creative acts.

Through creativity we confront our mortality; we experience resurrection and make it possible for the result of our creative act to live on beyond us, be it a child, a poem, project or idea.

I think we should take a vow of creativity, the vow to allow our imaginations to act in ways that we have not planned. The creative process is like parenting a child: first you give it life; then you give it love; and then you let it go. One of the reasons creativity is so challenging for us is that we want to control what we create. Parents know that is impossible. The same is true of a relationship. It is also true of a book or any project: you have no control over how it is understood. Creativity involves the most profound act of surrender we can engage in, allowing something to pass *through* us. It's such a paradoxical experience, because we have to be fully involved and out of the way at the same time: prolonged engagement and surrender. We don't own the results of our creative acts. We don't own our imagination or what our imagination gives birth to.

I remember the last basket that Michael Jordan shot for the Chicago Bulls. Here he was, right out there, and it was as if everything stopped, like slow motion. And all of a sudden ... *swish.* Some call that *flow.* Some call that *being in the zone.* It doesn't happen only in athletics but can appear in any part of our life: making love, making music, making stories. Being "in the zone" is when we totally forget ourselves and yet remain totally conscious of the moment. That is creativity. That is self-transcendence. The theological word for this is *resurrection.* Out of death life comes; out of nothingness newness is born.

Creativity as Healing

Creativity is an instrument of healing in our lives and for the planet. Perhaps the most healing gesture that we can make is to imagine that we belong. Belonging heals the deep wound of homelessness – the original alienation upon which is predicated the conviction that we are destined for a lifetime of therapy, a lifetime of pursuing many modalities of healing –because at some profound level we are convinced that we are unhealable, eternally without a home. A friend told me that one day she awoke convinced that the capacity to imagine is at the heart of healing. I believe she was right. Creativity makes healing possible because it challenges us to visualize what our life could be like if we no longer had the physical, emotional and spiritual limitations that keep us dis-eased.

I recall again now a pear tree we had in our backyard in my hometown in Canada. I learned two things from that tree: if you pick a pear too early, it isn't any good; if you leave it on the tree too long, it gets soft and rots. That was a lesson about creativity. There's a moment, a *timing,* in the creative process. Ideas need to ripen in us before they can be born. The idea of wellness needs to ripen in us before we can be healed. Creativity heals the hole in our troubled hearts; it is central to our human vocation.

The scriptures say we need to become children again; we do that by retrieving our imaginations. It is a mystical experience. It is an experience that is nourished by support and freedom and which results in healing for ourselves and our planet.

Wisdom and Creativity

As our traditions have retreated from relevance, spirituality has erupted in the minds and hearts of people. As faith in institutions has decreased, spirituality has increased. We have a great opportunity now. We have the opportunity to give birth to a new culture, to create not just with paintbrush but on the "canvas" of relationships. We can create a society in which women's voices are honoured, indigenous peoples are revered, traditions are revitalized, and science becomes mysticism rather than materialism. We need a new vision that will evoke positive energy, that will celebrate mystery, that will respond to the incredible hunger that we have for meaning in our lives. Thus consciousness and conscience become compatible. In a re-sacralized world silence and listening will be as reverenced. The prophetic voice will become our own, and we will have the creativity and the courage to express it.

At this critical point in human history, it is time to realize that ambiguity is probably the clearest approach we can take to describe who we are in this time of accelerated change. M.C. Richards brought this into focus for me. When asked to talk about herself, this brilliant woman, widely known for her book on creativity entitled *Centering*, explained that ambiguity is the best strategy to use to describe oneself. It is a way to avoid labels or stereotypes. If you label yourself by saying, "I am a doctor, or a lawyer, or a priest," you immediately become the cultural icon for that profession with all its limits and expectations. If, however, you announce yourself with a level of ambiguity, your true self will emerge and your creative potential will be more fully realized. On a societal level, in these in-between times, clarity becomes a fundamentalism and results in the positing of absolutes where they do not exist. As mentioned by Diarmuid O'Murchu in the Introduction, this is instead a time to live with messiness and to accept that from the chaos will emerge new forms that will give focus to our lives.

It is a time to ponder what the divine wants us to create in this moment of history. As I've noted before, Thomas Berry calls this a moment of grace, a moment where transformation is possible, where disruption provides opportunity rather than reasons for despair. It is a time to ingest the universe story, by reading, by reflection, by ritual, and by a new kind of literacy that sees in the natural world the face of the divine. It is a time to realize that we need to let go of the world view upon which much of our society has been based. Out of this shattering of the dominant world view the possibility for new life will emerge.

The Twilight of the Clockwork God by J.D. Ebert is a series of interviews with six eminent scientists. The book reminds us that we live in the last days of the "clockwork god," the god who was the mechanic with the oil can and whose prized possession was Detroit, because it made machines and automobiles. It is also a time to risk being on the edge of institutions but at the centre of issues. The power position is no longer at the White House or the Chancery Office or the City Hall but in the neighbourhoods and streets of the city, where people dare to talk about what is really important. It is a time to face our fears – of not belonging, of rejection, of success, of suffocation, of heights, of God. To face our fear is to ingest a hope that will take us into a future – a future of silence and listening. It is time for us to articulate a spirituality that will take us into tomorrow, sensitive to the pain of the planet, nourished by the beauty of creation, embraced by the divine presence in all of life. The new spirituality sees our primary impulse as one to create a better world for the offspring and the unborn of every species.

A Vision for Tomorrow

I picture the future as a planetary Pentecost. In the Christian tradition, Pentecost was the birth of the church – the birth of a new community of relationships and new life. This New Story also can give birth to a new community of life. Years ago in England, toward the end of the Second World War, Vera Lynn popularized a song called "When the Lights Go on Again All over the World." At the time, people were terrified that lights would make their homes targets for bombers. I suggest that it is time to turn the lights on – the lights of creativity and compassion, the lights of relationship and hope, the lights of a new awakening community.

We need to look at the relationship between intimacy and contemplation. In popular culture, as well as in our personal lives, there is probably a lack of one of these. We need both intimacy, so that our soul doesn't dry up, and enough silence and contemplative time in which to grow our soul. Edward Schillebeeckx, OP, describes this dynamic when he writes, "Without mysticism, politics soon becomes cruel and barbaric; without political love, mysticism becomes sentimental or uncommitted interiority." If we can balance the two, I think that we have the key to a lifestyle that fosters both spiritual development and a peaceful world.

A new mystical and engaged cosmology will re-energize our traditions and make them more relevant. We need cultural, as well as personal, therapy. We need to *deconstruct* society, to return to our point of origin. Then we need to *reconstruct* our society with the ethical principles that the universe teaches us: to respect difference, honour interiority and inwardness, and promote relationship and community. That is the task of the new cosmology; I call it *geo-justice*. Taking the dynamics of evolution, putting them into cultural form, and practising them provides us with a template for justice. The universe teaches us about ethics. If we truly made use of those principles, perhaps we wouldn't need the Ten Commandments. Only then would our vision of tomorrow become one of harmony, balance and peace.

> *When it's over, I want to say all my life I was a bride married to amazement.*
> *I was the bridegroom, taking the world into my arms.*
>
> —Mary Oliver

Threshold Moments

Find my voice
Respond to the impulse that lies deep within
Live at the threshold and precipice of unknowing
Go beyond the predictability of life
Stand at "the doorway of the unexpected"
Transcend moments of restlessness and compulsion

Embrace the revelatory moment
Stand still enveloped in the solitude of existence
Discover what it means to be free
Irrigate the soul and embrace the fault lines of my heart!!

Contemplation and Soul: Action/Reflection

How is your heart opened and your soul stirred as you contemplate the awe and wonder of the universe and the galaxies of your soul?

In what ways has the experience of intimacy and solitude enhanced your capacity to give full and conscious attention to your experience of ultimate mystery?

How through moments of contemplation, trusting your body, being willing to engage with others and embracing the present moment, have you been able to overcome the fear that blocks your capacity to experience the inmost recesses of your soul and to find your place in community?

What actions will energize and enhance your capacity to respond to the longing for intimacy and contemplation that resides in the universe and in your own soul?

Rediscovering Soul

To truly discover who we really are we must engage in a search:

- For a sacrament of engagement where our work for equality and justice becomes an act of love;

- For the subtle presence of the divine, who, as we discover with our new awareness, is already there;

- For a new sensitivity to the poor and oppressed whose vulnerability somehow reveals a transparency that allows the divine presence to shine through;

- To penetrate and transform the negative energy and bitterness that look like justice and are so often present in the struggle;

- To extend our internal sensitivity beyond self to embrace the other and the earth;

- To savour silence and discover there increased clarity, focus and self-esteem;

- To discover the currents of deep inner wisdom that foster our attentiveness to dreams, imagination and the unspoken language of God;

- For increased energy in the struggle, an enhanced sense of community and the time to explore a greater sense of purpose;

- To heal the hunger in the emptiness and recognition in relationship;

- For a deeper meaning of "animateur" – soul workers who are willing to risk, to slow down, go deeper, light a candle to dispel the darkness and bring beauty back to the world;

- For an increased capacity to live with mystery, with not knowing, and to find a resilient spirit even in broken dreams, loneliness, and the massive bureaucracy that often clouds our work;

- For our generational task, to discover soul in the Great Work as we listen attentively to the little ones of God and discover there a mystical cosmology that will nurture engagement and a culture of hope.

2

Longing of Life

A Canticle to Life

We awaken, as if for the first time, to life as primary sacrament;

- To a new life of cosmology, ecology, community and wisdom.

- To a life of reciprocity, gratefulness and awe.

- To a life of cosmic common vision, creativity and reverence.

- To a life of natural beauty, mysticism, and opportunity for the Great Work and integral presence.

- To a life that is holistic, that sees with new eyes the "divine goodness" everywhere.

- To a life where education is a spiritual practice that celebrates both intimacy and contemplation.

- To a life where we witness and therefore become.

- To a life whose culture is being brought to boil in and through the cosmological imagination that bursts forth from the heart of humanity and the heart of the cosmos itself.

- To a world of gratitude for "good companions on the way" and the awakening hunger for life that resides in the hearts of the young.

- To a new world that we can call home, a vision that will energize the next generation so that we can become a people of gratitude and glory for all that has been, is, and will be.

In this new life
- we will marry mind and the soul, the cognitive and the moral;
- our hearts and minds will go to the edge of our longing;
- we will respond to our unspoken hungers for sacredness and depth.

Together we will give birth to
- a re-enchanted cosmos,
- a new liberating cosmology, an operative contextual cosmology,
- a new genesis,
- a new civilization,
- a new moment of grace,
- a new Paschal moment,
- a new sense of destiny founded on a sustainable future where peace with earth makes possible peace on earth in a simultaneous embrace,
- a peace that is possible through an enduring journey of courage, joy, celebration and ecstasy.

Only then can we truly say that we are turning enthusiastically for home.

Home to our soul,
Home to life,
Home to Earth,
Home to the Divine.

Problems in life are not solved logically on their own terms but fade when confronted with a new and stronger life urge.

—Carl Jung

*I will always begin by listening... opening all my ears. I want to
listen to people's experience and only then do I apply critical analysis.*
—M.D. Chenu, OP

Longing of Life/Liberation

To become vulnerable, to experience deeply, to risk rejection
and allow our souls to grow with exposure to beauty, wonder and
surprise will bring us more fully to the edge of our longing for life.
It is here that our heart cries out. The poet Rilke writes, "Flare up
like a flame and make big shadows I can move in." As our hearts
ignite with passion, all that is hidden will emerge. We reach out and
open ourselves to relationship, to life. In our vulnerability we
embrace paradox, beauty and terror, and dance courageously into
the depths of self-discovery and life. With Rilke we say

Nearby is the country they call life.
You will know it by its seriousness.
Give me your hand.

A compass guides us on our journey into life. The Longing of
Life explores a new sense of freedom in relationship to class, race,
gender and creation.

*In the contemporary understanding, Christian life includes taking a
critical look at society, entering into solidarity with the marginalized
and excluded.*

—Gregory Baum

*Liberation theology's greatest contribution was its refocusing of
attention on the plight of the poor as a fundamental theological issue
and its encouragement of a spirituality centered on the struggle for
liberation from its various oppressions, especially from so-called social
sins.*

—Ivone Gebara

Creation is the first act of liberation.

—Gustavo Gutierrez

*What liberation theologians are saying today, and many others too,
is that the theologian must be involved (engagé as the French say).*
—Albert Nolan

*Prophetic (i.e. liberation) spirituality focuses on the struggle to restore
just and harmonious relations over against a world dominated by
great systems of oppression and injustice.*
—Rosemary Radford Ruether

*Each new difference is an expression of the unlimited potential that is
unfolding out of God's Word...Thus God's power to initiate unlimited
realities is coded directly into the creation process.*
—McGregor Smith

*All social justice issues have ecological implications...The cry of the
earth and the cry of the poor are one.*
—Pastoral letter on the Christian Ecological
Imperative from the Social Affairs Commission,
Canadian Catholic Conference of Bishops

Reflection: Our quest for life, for freedom involves taking on a new identity, becoming a new species; from this perspective our focus is not only the liberation of humanity, but the liberation of life itself; we take up that challenge of a preferential option for the poor and the poor earth.

Liberation and Life

*Gratitude and grace
Epiphanies of freedom
Speaking truth to power
Transforms how it feels to be free.*

Moments of Sacredness and Depth

Vulnerability: Taking Down the Umbrella of Our Lives

To become vulnerable, to experience deeply, to risk rejection and allow our souls to grow with exposure to beauty, wonder and surprise will bring us more fully to the edge of our longings. It is here that our heart cries out in pursuit of life. As the poet Rilke writes, "Flare up like flame and make big shadows I can move in." As our defences melt, our hearts ignite more fully with passion; all that is hidden will emerge. As we reach out further into life we open ourselves and renew our commitment to relationship, to people and places that have captured our hearts and fuelled our journey. In our vulnerability we embrace paradox, beauty and terror, and dance courageously into the depths of self-discovery, where we are able to proclaim together with Rilke,

> *Near is the land which they call life.*
> *You will know it by its earnestness.*
> *Give me your hand.*

And so we journey with openness and trust into the uncharted future. With gratitude and praise we celebrate each precious moment, each opportunity to quench our thirst for life. These eternal longings are the compass for the journey that, as Teilhard de Chardin puts it, we "dare to call our life." This interior compass guides us forward into the depths of our emotional truth. A compass, unlike a map that already has the destination marked out, continues to guide us through an ever-changing and unfolding journey.

A New Meaning for a Listening Heart

> *Our heart is that center where we are one with ourselves,*
> *with all others, and with God....*
> *A listening heart perceives meaning.*

> —Br. David Steindl-Rast

My brother phoned. He had received the results of his catheterization and the diagnosis was not good: he would be undergoing triple-bypass surgery in the morning. As we talked, questions, fear and memories tumbled into my consciousness. Suddenly I was transported back to my adolescence and recalled with stark vividness the desolation I felt at my mother's funeral. As my brother spoke of his possible death, I felt the "buffer" between myself and mortality torn away. And when he asked to "talk to me about something spiritual," my sense of inadequacy reached a high peak. As we spoke that evening, questions of pain, suffering, death, prayer and personal conscience tumbled into the conversation. It was the most intimate and meaningful exchange in all our decades of life. On the eve of open-heart surgery my brother's heart opened as never before. Long before the surgeon's incision, he was changed. Time, children, marriage and the preciousness of existence swelled with greater value. It was a powerful lesson for the entire family: when we face death, we embrace life.

As I pondered these life-changing events, I recalled the wisdom of Saul Alinsky, the architect of community organization, who decades ago had reminded us that when we have a heart attack or some other serious illness, our values change, and what seemed important before does not matter now:

> Suddenly it came to me...as a gut revelation, that someday I was going to die.... Once you accept your own mortality, on the deepest level, your life can take on a whole new meaning...you won't care any more how much money you've got or what people think of you...whether you're successful or unsuccessful, important or insignificant. You just care about living every day to the full, drinking in every new experience and sensation as eagerly as a child, and with the same sense of wonder.

With my brother's post-operative prognosis good, and his recovery well underway, his children, siblings and spouse were left to reflect on the lessons that lie on the threshold of death. The card I sent to him immediately after his surgery read: "Friends who plant kindness gather love." Inside I wrote:

Dear Bob:

This card says it all. These days have reminded us of how precious you are and how precious life is. The next stage of your journey will be richer, deeper and more joyful. Thank you for your courage and your life. I'm glad you're well.
Love,
Jim

I continue to distil the wisdom from these turbulent days and realize, perhaps for the first time, that to encounter mortality is to begin life anew.

There is a wisdom in listening to our traditions, to the world. By listening our assumptions can be challenged and our perspectives broadened. By listening we can discover there is reason to hope. By listening we can discover that changing the world is possible.
—Parliament of World Religions

Our listening creates a sanctuary for the homeless parts within the other person.
—Rachel Naomi Remen

The Cradle of Connectedness

Waiting for the voice that may desire to speak from the depths of its own silent listening.
—Paulo Freire

The great prophetic Brazilian educator Paulo Freire wrote, "The space of the democratic-minded teacher who learns to speak by listening is interrupted by the intermittent silence of his or her own capacity to listen, waiting for that voice that may desire to speak from the depths of its own silent listening." I was reminded again as I reflected on the effects in me of my brother's illness; the willingness to listen, to learn, to change, to be vulnerable, to engage deeply, with the emanation of one's or another's heart is at the centre of our longings. Silence makes it possible to be committed to the experience of communication, to hear the questions, the doubt, the creativity of the person who is speaking, and to discover our own voice.

Listening and recognition, as I wrote in chapter one, are the greatest gifts we can give to another, and also to ourselves. Their practise invites intimacy, makes communication possible, energizes the spirit and creates a context, a fertile silence to foster wisdom. To listen is a permanent attitude of being open to the word of the other, to the gesture of the other, to the difference of the other. Listening requires a generous, loving heart, respect, tolerance, humility, joy, love, and openness to what is new, to what is welcome, to change, to perseverance, to struggle, to hope and to justice. Listening gives access to what is eternally true, to the heart of wisdom, of liberation, of creation. It flows from a conviction that life is ours to create. By listening we can satisfy the longing for intimacy, the cravings of our soul for life.

A Passion for Justice

Those who train many in the ways of justice will sparkle like the stars for all eternity.

—The Book of Daniel

It was eleven o'clock on a Chicago morning in May, 2001. The funeral mass for Monsignor John J. Egan had just concluded; the procession would soon be on its way to the cemetery. Though I was in Berkeley, I found myself imagining standing there on the sidewalk surrounded by many who had loved and learned from him, remembering with deep feelings of gratitude and loss the great man who had left us.

I had met Jack Egan at Notre Dame more than three decades before. As I sat in his office that day wondering about my future, the telephone rang often. On the line were people from the justice community of the American Catholic Church like Dan Berrigan, Gino Baroni, Dorothy Day, Kathy Kelly or Margie Tuite. Each had a personal connection to the man Andrew Greeley called "the midwife of every significant Catholic Action initiative in our era."

Jack became a friend and advocate, a person whose sensitivity to the needs of the poor and powerless boiled over into a passionate commitment to justice and civil rights for all. Jack had the capacity to make you feel like you belonged. He spread his gospel of "information, support, and the possibility of common action" to all who were asea in the turbulent years of the post–Vatican II church. He was ahead of his time, behind every issue that hoped for and promised justice. He was sensitive, even easily hurt, yet profoundly attuned to the pain of the marginalized, to those who have no voice. Tim Unsworth captured the essence of Monsignor Egan in his book *The Last Priests in America: Conversations with Remarkable Men:* "Jack Egan remains the consummate communicator. He is the master of the short but pointed letter and the perfectly aimed phone call." It is his gift of passion for justice for which I'll remember him the most, a passion that made a difference in my life and the lives of so many more. I also remember his personal kindness and support when I really needed it.

He spent time with me at Notre Dame University when I flew in unexpectedly for a visit. He wrote to the bishop to express his support for my ministry. He made it possible for me to participate in the Urban Training Center for Christian Mission and the Industrial Area's Foundation Saul Alinsky Training Institute in Chicago, both pivotal experiences for me. He invited me onto the board of the Catholic Committee on Urban Ministry and supported my work as Canadian liaison.

Most of all, he was a man who believed in people and made it possible for us to believe in ourselves. He was a good man, a good friend, a good priest – I still miss him.

> *Father Jack Egan believed he could best serve God by serving all of God's people here in Chicago and across the globe. Their aspirations for justice became his agenda for a life of service... Today Jack would ask each of us, "What are you doing for justice?"*
>
> —Peggy Roach

Priesthood – Yesterday and Tomorrow

> *In our loneliness, comfort us; in our sorrows, strengthen us. Give us a deep faith in others, in ourselves, and in You...a bright, firm hope which will even increase in the journey to You, who is the journey. Dare we thank you, God, for our pain, if it leads to Your open embrace? Amen.*
>
> —Fr. Bill O'Donnell

The television news portions out its toxic reports – pedophilia is an epidemic across the country. Accusations abound toward the ordained ones, the perpetrators of this profound pain.

Pain for the little ones, and pain for an institution that reels from accusations as the secrets too long held become known. Broken lives exposed on the small screen for everyone to see, a clerical culture has imploded on itself. No longer a member of a caste system identified by symbol and secrecy, today's priest has traded in his cassock of honour for a cloak of suspicion, which he now wears in the public mind, even if not personally warranted.

A false consciousness of other-worldliness and the illusion of being "a little less than the angels" have mercifully been debunked. Arrested moral and psychological development is agonizingly manifest for all to see in the acts of betrayal and self-serving lies.

Perhaps now the priesthood can turn back to its essentials, turn toward a new time when, like a phoenix, it will rise from the shackles of domination and abuse to a place of renewed humanity without illusion, pretence or privilege,

To a place of service and sacrifice.

To a place where distrust is overcome, meaning rediscovered, destiny restored.

To a place where fresh energy carries us beyond the limitations of measured giving.

To a place where gratitude and gestures of generosity are integral to the fabric of existence.

To a place where relationship and an experience of communion are celebrated in a holy and wholesome way.

To a place where trust is restored and the innocence of the little ones is respected.

Perhaps then we will discover in relationship to all a new experience of community that gives meaning to being "sacerdote" for our time.

A Time for Healing

My help is in the mountain
Where I take myself to heal
The earthly wounds
 that people give to me.
I find a rock with sun on it

And a stream where the water runs gently
And the trees one by one give me company.

—Nancy Wood

The Monks of Skid Row

A strange breed of monks, these
12,000 derelicts of life,
these loveable genial isolated human
beings.
They live with a past not to be
forgotten,
a present built out of isolation,
and a future that promises and hopes
for nothing.
These monks of the inner city are
more alone
than the strictest contemplative —
and often more redeemed
as they traffic in their currency of
cigarettes,
where to get beer, a bed, a meal, a
job and sometimes money.
They are selfless and concerned,
these islands of humanity boasting of
a day's work and regretting a wasted life.
They trust NO ONE as they walk
their silent world of pain and fear,
this order of the street, people without
futures, without rights.
Poor, pushed, passed by, and
possessed
by those who provide beds and food,
keeping them on one aimless treadmill
of life.
They live without solutions,
with no one listening to what they say,

71

no one asking them to talk,
 inviting them to spill, to drain
the poison from their lives —
a poison that festers in nightmares,
alcohol,
fear of work, passive acceptance of
mistreatment,
unexpressed anger and fear.

"Don't Forget the Tenderloin"

How can I help but think of these things every time I sit down at
Chrystie Street or Peter Maurin Farm and look at the tables filled
with the unutterably poor who are going through their long-
continuing crucifixion?

…The mystery of the poor is this:

that they are Jesus and what you do for them you do for Him….

The mystery of poverty is that by sharing in it,

making ourselves poor in giving to others,

we increase our knowledge of and belief in love.

—Dorothy Day

Mary Ann Finch invited us to gather in a circle. As music filled the room, we followed her lead into movement and song. She woke up our bodies so the spirit could also rise.

She reminded me of Dorothy Day, who inspired generations to live lives of voluntary poverty and service to the poor. Mary Ann told us of her Care Through Touch Institute where the inner city of San Francisco was her classroom, and her receptive heart a home for those whose lives are "pushed and passed by" by those who, adorned in white shirts, suits and attaché cases, strive to ignore or escape the gaze of the crucified ones who live in the streets. These are the victims of a cruel system that insures the economic achievements of some and the exclusion of others. They are people whose lives are witness to an economy predicated on unfair labour practices resulting in a growing number of urban and environmental refugees.

But in our circle there was a spirit of joy and playfulness inspired by Mary Ann, who dares to see the suffering Christ in abandoned and displaced people and discovers there a monastery to heal the sacred longings of our cultural soul.

Later on Holy Thursday a group of us joined Mary Ann and her colleagues to repeat the generosity of Jesus on the first Holy Thursday – The Last Supper. Taking his act of service as an example, we massage the feet of the homeless in the ghetto of San Francisco.

One of the people I was privileged to meet there was the elderly woman originally from Massachusetts whose story, when I first touched her feet, began to flow from her. It was a story of broken relationships and broken dreams, a lifetime of longing to be accepted and loved.

As we parted, I was grateful for the experience with the woman of the Tenderloin: it was "a Eucharist of compassion," a Passover moment for each of us.

On another occasion, it was Thanksgiving Day; a group of us again joined along with The Little Brothers of Jesus and Friends of the Elderly to deliver food, drink and flowers to the elderly people living in single rooms in old hotels in San Francisco's inner city. Here we met people hidden away in their crowded quarters. They were grateful for the gifts we brought and more so for the contact we provided.

As I left San Francisco that day I knew that the memory of Mary Ann and her friends would remain and that along with many others I would not forget the Tenderloin.

Like every human being who hungers and thirsts for justice and peace, Dorothy Day had periods of complete exhaustion, sorrow, and pain. I was told that she would then withdraw and cry – for hours and days.... When I discovered this, I understood better what pacifism is, what God means in the midst of defeat, how the spirit comforts us and leads us into truth.

—Dorothee Soelle

73

Gestures of the Heart

In the beginner's mind there are many possibilities...
—Shunryu Suzuki-Roshi

The following event took place on Immersion Day at Sophia Center, a time when the students begin the semester by visiting the homeless and displaced people of San Francisco's inner city.

We exited the BART (Bay Area Rapid Transit) station and hurried to St. Boniface Church in San Francisco's "Tenderloin District" to begin our day with the city's homeless. We discovered there "the home" of 28,000 people living in a 14-square block area, a district bordered by the power structures of this internationally recognized city nestled on the San Francisco Bay: the Civic Center (political), Nob Hill (social) and Union Square (commercial).

As Mary Ann Finch of the Care Through Touch Institute (a program that provides massage and support for the people of the Tenderloin) welcomed us to our "urban plunge," we became palpably aware of the love that is extended to and expressed daily by these "little ones of God," these people of the Tenderloin who spend their days sleeping in the park, waiting for a meal and bouncing around the health care system in an often futile attempt to receive medical attention. These "little ones," these homeless ones are consistently sheltered by the open hearts of those who each day befriend and dissolve the terror of exile and alienation that festers in the cell blocks of the street.

As we stood in line that day and joined the multitude who are served meals daily by St. Anthony's Foundation, stories of pain, isolation and yet great dignity were told; narratives of broken lives and shattered dreams poured forth, prompted not only by physical hunger but also a deeper longing for meaning, purpose, pride and life. Yet amidst the many sacred stories we heard that day, we felt with ever greater cadence pulsations of compassion from those who society seems too willing to discard.

On our day in the Tenderloin we went back to school. In our inner-city classroom we discovered as if for the first time that joy lives in the streets where we were introduced to homeless persons; they became our teachers, our mentors and our guides. As they introduced us to the agencies and people who serve the Tenderloin, we were gifted with more stories: stories of remarkable courage, stories of beauty and brokenness, gestures of the heart that heal pain and build bridges of friendship.

To complete the day, we gathered in a circle; our teachers with great gratitude and moving pride shared their experiences of the day. This sacred event transcended previous moments of broken marriages, rejection by families, endless nights on park benches, untreated illness and multiple addictions. At that moment we were enveloped in a membrane of hope and love. In this circle of compassion our teachers taught us again to laugh, to listen and to cry. They taught us to transcend the symbols of power that surround "the Tenderloin" and permeate our lives; they reminded us that "God is present in the poor." We discovered from our teachers that divinity lives in the Tenderloin and other places of poverty, and that its address can be found in gestures of the heart.

As we returned to the street and entered the nearest BART station, the lyrics of our "song of the day" echoed in our hearts:

"I will never leave you
I will always love you
I will always keep you in my heart."

Mother of the Streets

I want to know how the child in you longs for home; that when you are frightened or alarmed "by people in the streets," remember it is a dimension of yourself that walks there, that lives without address and documented identity and perhaps spent last night in a "cardboard condo" in a park, a storefront or in the rain.

I want you to know that your mother is with you on your journey; accepts, embraces, loves you, and welcomes you home to her heart.

A welcoming heart, a heart of hospitality that feels the pain of unclean needles, the pain of exile and alienation, the pain of rejection by self, other and the world.

I want you to know that my heart is always open, that my arms embrace you, as my hands offer you bread-for-the-journey — it is the bread of hospitality and nourishment of home.

I want you to know that I am present with you in the streets, that you and your lifestyle are as dignified and worthy as those whose picket fences and gated communities keep out the public, the pain of the people and also me.

I want you to know that this is a place of connectedness, that this is your home and that the many relationships of the street are the monasteries of your life.

I want you to know that no matter where you are, wherever you sleep, however homeless you may feel, that the street itself is a sacred place, a place for life, a place of nobility, a place of peace where people, good people and your Mother of the Streets also dwell.

I want you to heal your wound of homelessness, your wound of exile and invite you to come home to yourself, to your friends, even to your pain and, of course, to the beautiful person that you are.

I want you to come home, home to the street, home to your God and home to your Mother of the Streets who welcomes you.

Come up on the Front Step and Tell Me a Story

I thank you and say how proud
    that I have been by fate allowed
To stand here having the joyful chance
    to claim my inheritance.

—Patrick Kavanaugh

Reflections on the Conlon Family Reunion: In his later years my father Richard would sit on the front porch of his home in Sombra and call out to those who passed by, "Come up on the porch, take a chair and tell me a story." And the people came, farmers in from the fields, neighbours from our village and others he had yet to meet.

In a similar way, we members of the Conlon family came to Port Lambton and Sombra to remember and tell our common story. It is a story enveloped in a membrane of ancestral memory. A story that began in 1844, when our ancestors left their homeland in

County Armagh, Ireland, and sailed to Ontario, Canada. . inscribed in the deep sadness of an oppressed people driven from their homeland by famine and oppression. It is a story recorded on the tombstones, in the cemeteries of Sombra and Port Lambton. It is a story told by the beauty of the St. Clair River, the first fall of snow that carpeted our fields in early winter, and by the leaves that adorned the big maple tree in our backyard with colours of gold, red and orange: a story told in many ways through the sacredness and wonder of this place.

As a child. I remember that my mother would participate in quilting bees. She would join a group of women in one of their homes and engage in their common project, the making of a quilt. In a similar way we gathered on the shores of the St. Clair to create together "The Conlon Quilt." From Alberta to Delaware, Virginia to California, New Hampshire to Michigan, Ontario to New Jersey, each of us a patch cut from common cloth held together by our shared ancestral thread, we became together "The Conlon Quilt."

Our family reunion has been a homecoming and a coming home to Sombra and Port Lambton, to ourselves, to each other, to this sacred place and to our God. When our ancestors came in from their farms to do their shopping they would ride in a horse and buggy. When it was time to return, they would point the horse towards home, and it would gallop off enthusiastically. It knew it was going home.

In a similar way at this reunion, we have experienced a fresh energy, because in coming here we knew that we were pointed toward home. We have responded to my father's invitation, "Come up here on the porch and tell me a story." It is a story we have heard from those who have gone before, a story that is now ours to tell to those who will follow. A story embedded in memories of front porches, quilting bees, church, cemeteries, natural beauty and home.

> *To live in the world*
> *You have to be able*
> *To do three things:*
> *To love what is mortal*
> *To hold it*

Against your bones knowing
Your own life depends on it
And, when the time comes, to let it go.
To let it go.

—Mary Oliver

Awakening in the Heart of Darkness

Who is our neighbour, the Samaritan? The outcast? The enemy? Yes,
yes, of course. We must love them all as ourself.

—Brian Patrick

Thoughts on September 11, 2001

It is 6:00 a.m. on a Tuesday; the streets in Berkeley are bathed in the light of dawn. Papers are delivered, coffee shops bustle, the "Y" greets early arrivals as BART (Bay Area Rapid Transit) hums its customary sound. It's "Morning in America."

Suddenly we become aware that the day is not as we had expected. Events are taking place that will change the course of history. Suicide bombers crash into the World Trade Center 18 minutes apart, felling the monetary icon of American capitalism. Soon afterwards, the Pentagon, the symbol of militarism, absorbs a similar shock. A fourth plane, apparently off-course, crashes into an open field in Pennsylvania.

America has been attacked on her own soil. She awakes from the deep sleep of her false security. No longer is she invincible in her global isolation. Her people suddenly feel a sense of imminent jeopardy. What has happened to the "good life," the budgetary surplus, and the feeling of planetary peace?

September 11, 2001, is a watershed moment in America. It has brought out the best and worst in people. This proud nation, stretching "from sea to shining sea," has become a village. For the moment, political ideology and radical strife have melted. We've become a country of compassion and citizens of solidarity. The tragedy of New York and Washington has reminded us of those we love and has given us a new appreciation of freedom.

It is also true that the danger of demonization hangs heavy in the air, like the clouds of smoke billowing from the ashes in Manhattan. Toxic theology and fundamentalist mantras have surfaced in the spiritual spectrum. A distorted perception of Christianity has misinterpreted these events as divine punishment for moral decay. An equally distorted view of Islam has blindly labelled a group of political fanatics as the representatives of this peace-loving tradition, making anyone who is a member of this faith a target for hatred and even death.

We desperately need to recover a spirituality of original goodness at this time when the events of this day's sunrise have given our moment a new name: "Mourning in America."

With tortured minds and wounded hearts, we ask what lies behind these atrocious acts of violence that render life cheap and sovereignty elusive. The questions tumble forth: Is it the isolationist policy of the "Ugly American" that props up foreign dictators only to demonize them at a later time? Is it the "global economy" whose "open" markets disadvantage two-thirds of the world, leaving those in poverty full of moral outrage at us, the privileged few? Is it our lack of leadership on the world stage, our "growth and greed" approach to deciding what is in America's best interest? What of the conflict over diminishing resources caused by our all-consuming greed for oil and commodification of the planet?

Perhaps a deeper question at this turning point in our history is this: How do we find a common cause as a people and a global family that will energize our efforts for peace? How do we support the common good to nurture a healthy planet with healthy people? Some ways are gathering in peace walks with your neighbours joining prayer and wisdom circles. Guidance can be found in the prophetic voices of Gandhi, Martin Luther King, Jr., Thich Nhat Hanh, Dan Berrigan, Barbara Lee, and the growing number whose non-violent protests, teach-ins, actions and projects of solidarity are weaving people from diverse faiths, traditions, races and regions into a fabric of peace.

The sun rose on Tuesday, September 11, to illuminate the ruins of American icons and the tragic loss of life. As a people we are called to discover a vision of possibility at this defining moment in our history.

Let us change our fundamental cultural story into a narrative of hope for the preservation of life.

Let us keep on believing in the fruitfulness of our efforts. Let us join with those who are willing to risk their lives and lifestyles that others may flourish and live. Let us become strong enough to listen to the poverty of a planet and a people in pain. Let us become courageous enough to work for renewed solidarity with all expressions of life.

Then we can nurture new expressions of compassion and co-create structures of peace. Then we can become fully present to those we love. Then we can nurture a new global spirituality and energize a world order of harmony, balance and peace.

So let us celebrate the Earth as a living community and our common home. Let us cultivate a spiritual practice of non-violence. Let us be willing to perform acts of kindness and love. Let us engage the sacredness of each moment and the capacity for a listening heart.

With that, we can discover from the depths of our collective consciousness fresh images of the divine. We can discover new levels of awareness that we are one living system touched by the same water, air, food and earth – and sustained by a common divinity. We can nurture a common vision of possibility that energizes and honours beauty, joy, goodness and truth.

From there we can continue to deepen and expand our spiritual journey by remembering our stories. Listen to the wisdom of creation, of the prophets, to the promptings of your hearts. Let go of anything that may stand in the way of realizing this vision of a possible future.

October 7, 2001 – The Response

It's Sunday, October 7th. The homilist at St. Joseph the Worker Church reads from Mark Twain's essay on the evils of war, including this quote:

> It was indeed a glad and gracious time, and the half
> dozen rash spirits that ventured to disapprove of the war

and cast a doubt upon its righteousness straightway got
such a stern and angry warning that for their personal
safety's sake they quickly shrank out of sight and
offended no more in that way.

The liturgy concludes; we return to the street and hear the news.
America has retaliated. Bombs are falling on Afghanistan.

The antiseptic language of the Pentagon masks the reality of
violence and death. Words crowd the airwaves: friendly fire,
collateral damage, infinite justice, enduring freedom. But over them
I hear Gandhi proclaim, "An eye for an eye leaves the whole world
blind."

As the hours creep by, the media's "manufactured consent" strives
to present a palatable version of this terrible moment. The television
screen becomes an apologist for destruction and death. Despite their
efforts, a growing number of people question the acts of aggression
that made our planet's poorest nation a target. We ask what religion
has to do with a war over a nation's national resources; we wonder
what role fundamentalism plays in the destruction of global peace.
We want to find out how a healthy spirituality can contribute to
planetary peace.

What response does this moment call for? What is the true
meaning of "peace"? Is war an obsolete vehicle for bringing beauty
and balance to the world? Can the practice of non-violence heal
this broken world? And in what way can each of us change, cleanse,
purify and protect the planet and its peoples at this time of
destruction and death?

In summary, we need to know how we can heal the "terrorist
paranoia" that harkens back to the Joseph McCarthy era and the
time of the House Un-American Activities Committee. What
strategies are available to us at the onset of this aimless war that
might prevent a repetition of the ambiguity of the Vietnam conflict,
a memory that remains painfully awash in our cultural soul? Where
do we look for guidance in the wake of Desert Storm, when a cycle
of violence strikes hardest at the poor and ravages our fragile planet?
What is required to nurture a culture of beauty and peace, and protect
it for future generations? What will remove the desire for permanent

conflict – the legacy of the Cold War – from the consciousness and conscience of America?

In this new "age of anxiety," amidst terrorist attacks and military retaliation, the words of Nobel Peace Prize winner Rigoberta Menchû Tum point us toward healing:

There will be no Peace if there is no Justice.
There will be no Justice if there is no Equity.
There will be no Equity if there is no Progress.
There will be no Progress if there is no Democracy.
There will be no Democracy if there is no Respect
For the Identity and Dignity of the Peoples and Cultures.

Seeking a True Meaning of Peace

"NO WAR ... PEACE!"

"Peace is not the product of terror or fear...
Peace is the generous tranquil contribution of all for the good of all."
—Oscar Romero

"In countries marked by grave injustice, joining the conflict,
not judging it from a distance,
is the only effective way of bringing about the peace that God wants."
—Albert Nolan, OP

Wednesday

It was Wednesday evening in mid-March; I arrived home and turned on the TV to hear the news and it was not good: bombs were falling on Iraq – the "war" had begun.

As I sat there stunned and disturbed at the events unfolding before me, I recalled a time in Costa Rica when many gathered from many countries to reflect on the question, "What is the true meaning of peace?" Sitting with pictures of destruction before me, I asked the question again, "What is peace?" Is it more than the absence of war? a state of mind? a way to relate?

Thursday

I joined hundreds of people who gathered for a candlelight vigil in Martin Luther King, Jr. Park in Berkeley to protest the war. A highlight of the evening occurred when Aidan, a five-year-old boy, appeared onstage at the "open mike." As he clutched the microphone and shouted "NO WAR!" we all responded "PEACE!"

He was soon whisked away by his parents and I imagined him being tucked lovingly into bed.

But his child's voice still resonated in the hearts and minds of those of us huddled together, holding our candles in the dark, this moment awakened in me thoughts of the children of Iraq who lie frightened and hungry, their young lives vulnerable both to the sanctions and to the bombs making their deadly trajectory from the sky.

Later, as I listened to a young man sing of peace and protest, the prophetic words of Pope Paul VI came to mind: "If *you* want peace, work for justice!" While pondering these words I asked, Does seeking the true meaning of peace ask us to

- **Disarm:** Not only in Iraq but also in our lives; to reduce any advantage of power, position or privilege as a parent, spouse, supervisor, city or nation?

- **Forgive:** Let go of any resentment toward the other: family member, co-worker, political or corporate leader, people from another race, country, gender or land?

- **Protect:** Shield the vulnerable ones: the child, the feelings of a friend, the beauty of creation, whether it means not drilling for oil, or remembering to recycle at home?

- **Revere:** Hold sacred the "little ones of God," the child, the elder, the dreams and aspirations of a people, and the sovereignty of a nation?

Saturday

People from many cities around the world were gathering in the streets to protest the pain, violence and terror of war. As I began the afternoon liturgy, the readings spoke to me of peace; the Woman at the Well reminded me of the thirst of a world that seeks the running waters of peace; the story of Jesus chasing the money-changers from the temple told of the greed that devalues people, plunders the earth, and makes nature's resources a reason for war.

As I reflected on these readings, at this mid-point in Lent, I saw in a new way that preparation for Easter is a preparation for peace: to disarm, forgive, protect and revere are ways to make our Easter and become resurrection people.

I recalled the first Easter and how Jesus, on the Road to Emmaus, greeted each with a gesture of peace: "Peace be with you." Perhaps today, in this new moment of anxiety, we can pray that the road to Baghdad, to Washington, to Ottawa, London, Paris, Moscow and Berkeley can become a road to peace, a road to truth, justice and love, a road to disarmament, forgiveness, protection and reverence.

As the Spirit speaks through the voices of the people who gather in solidarity and outrage on behalf of a defenceless people in a defenceless land, a new Pentecost, a Pentecost of peace is being born. May it flow down from the Euphrates and Tigris, to the Rideau Canal, to the Potomac, the current centres of power. May it create a harmony of heart, a new beatitude, a declaration of love, and a dream yet to be realized.

It is a response to the voice of little Aidan and the voices of all children ringing in our ears:

NO WAR, PEACE!
NO WAR, PEACE!
NO WAR, PEACE!

"Even as we gaze over the grimy world before us, the sun shines radiantly over the earth ... We participate in the original dream of the earth.

Where else can we go for the guidance needed for the task that lies before us."
– Thomas Berry

It's Already Gone Off

The bomb has already gone off.
In Kosovo, Afghanistan, Ground Zero,
Oklahoma City, Iraq and more.
In the rainforests of Brazil,

The waters of the Ganges,
The fields that give us food.

The bomb has already gone off
In the hearts of the mad bombers,
In the souls of our children,
In the heart of the Earth.
The bomb has already gone off!

April, 2003: You Can't Make Your Easter with Your Back to Baghdad

Television news and the print media bring home to us the dark clouds billowing up in the oil fields and the ruined infrastructure of the fragile cradle of civilization today known as the country of Iraq.

We ask ourselves today, "How can we peer through the darkness; the darkness of smoke, of violence, of fear, of greed, of devastation and death, and find there a light of hope and rebirth to illuminate our perspective on war and the pain and destruction that accompany it?"

In the middle of Lent as the invasion of Iraq occurs, I ask, "How can the mad bombers of Calvary leads us to the empty tomb of new life?" "How can the palpable presence of the divine, embedded in the poor people of Iraq, become manifest in the torn landscape of their people?"

With these questions in mind I remember the promise of Oscar Romero who proclaimed, "If they kill me, I will rise in the people of El Salvador."

I recall the words of Johannes Metz who wrote, "You can't do theology with your back to Auschwitz."

As I ponder these prophetic utterances and the times in which we live, these words came to me as a mantra for this critical moment: "You can't make your Easter with your back to Baghdad."

A Second Exodus – Of Peace

In the wake of September 11, 2001, we entered a new age of anxiety and another era, the "Age of the Aftershock." This is a time when the violence perpetrated against America and our response have unleashed a series of events punctuated by acts of violence and consumer madness.

Among these are

- The bombing of land and people in Afghanistan that began in October, 2001.

- The Enron debacle that revealed the depth and proliferation of a culture of "greed and growth" which has infected the economic integrity of our nation.

- The pedophilia crisis that has revealed the violation of many children, a crucifixion of soul that has scandalized many and diminished the moral authority of the Church.

- The sniper craze that erupted in the Washington, D.C., area, propelling waves of meaningless death onto many innocent citizens.

- Episodic outbreaks of violence on campuses and in classrooms where schools, teachers and classmates become the victims of violent outbursts and self-inflected wounds.

- The demonization and duplicity enveloped in politics and the media.

- The continuing sabre-rattling in the Middle East where the mad bombers of the West continue a campaign of nuclear and ecological apartheid against the planet and the people who dwell in this ancestral home.

As the long arm of the West reaches to possess the spigot of oil and rob a sovereign nation of its natural resources, I reflect on the unjust aggression that is being unleashed against our fragile planet earth. I ponder how water, the new blue gold, has become so widely polluted that 80 per cent of illness is caused by the toxic impact on water supplies, the world's circulatory system. The result is that "the blood of Earth" can no longer act as an authentic sacrament of new life nor healthfully quench the thirst of humanity and every species.

Similarly, as the recipient of toxins and radioactive material due to war and careless waste management, the land is diminished in its capacity to nurture health and bring forth food for all.

The atmosphere has also become a vehicle of poison and respiratory illness, relinquishing its capacity to invigorate our bodies and become the oxygen of our souls, a resource whereby we can transcend all depression and sweep aside the despair that has made us the most medicated country in the world.

Meanwhile, our nearest kin, the animals, have become victims of extinction and diseases, deprived of habitat, adequate nourishment, and a place to raise their young.

As the outbreak of aggression began in Iraq, I thought that as a people we are being called to engage in a "Second Exodus," a deep transition, a transformative moment toward peace, not only to heal the hot spots on our endangered planet, but also to permeate all aspects of soul, life and creation.

This "Second Exodus" will occur when we rediscover fire and water. Fire, to permeate the darkness of our time and reactivate our collective memory of the original fire that is the continuing source of all energy and life. Water, as an archetypal source and symbol of new life to quench our thirst for sacredness and depth and reinvigorate with vitality and fresh energy the planet and its people.

We realize that peace, planetary peace, will involve multiple gestures of generosity and the willingness to transcend the bitter and burdensome aspects of life.

Such peace will nurture

- A country of compassion, a society of solidarity, and a new gratitude for freedom.

- A renewed appreciation of globalization that will embrace human rights and ecological justice.

- A transformation of the growth and greed ideology toward a new appreciation of sovereignty and the inherent value of all.

- The capacity to rewrite our story into a narrative of hope that will bring forth a society of presence.

"Longing for Running Waters"

God of the Cosmos,
Source of Mystery and Life,
Quench our thirst.

Pour out your living waters
On all who long for life.
On the parched landscape of the Middle East.
On all the peoples who hunger
And thirst for acceptance,
For health, home and bread.
On all who cry out for
Beauty, truth and justice.
On all who gather here today
On the shores of the Pacific
People of diverse traditions and creeds
United in a common concern for creation
Our beautiful and fragile earth.
Quench our thirst for hope,
Our longing for peace, for mystery,
For life.

A Second Superpower – For Planetary Peace

Today the world's children are in even more desperate agony; bodies maimed by our landmines, poisoned by waste from our nuclear warheads, starved to death by our embargos; minds maimed by violence in our media, poisoned by our warped value system, starved because we filch from education what we waste on war. Yet today as always the fierce compassion of mothers – of the mother in each of us – rises defiantly to defend the world's hope: the world's children.

It is the calm determination of the mother's sheltering embrace that makes this image an icon of hope for me. Please look at it long enough to feel not only the agony, but also the hope. When, this past March, millions around the world rose up to cry out for peace, a new "superpower," as the New York Times called it, made itself heard.

This time the cry was stifled, but a new year will offer us new opportunities. Let us pledge to act for change and act in hope.

—Br. David Steindl-Rast, OSB

With each passing decade and day, conflict in Iraq and the Middle East becomes increasingly the epicentre of a culture both withered and destroyed. As the faces and names of the fallen are announced in the news, there is a growing consensus that this cultural moment, marked by pre-emption and occupation, has eroded the founding vision of a people based on freedom and hope.

As Dante needed Virgil in order to descend into the Inferno and return liberated and free, we as a people require the strength and healing properties of a new religious/spiritual sensitivity to confront destructiveness in our midst and emerge as the people of a planetary peace.

Years ago Richard Price, co-founder of Esalen Institute in Northern California, underwent many insulin-shock treatments to resolve a pathology that invaded his soul. When at Esalen, he was able to discharge his toxic emotions and achieve a life of balance and peace. After his death his friends gathered at a memorial service and recited his mantra:

> *His life was full of pain.*
> *At first it drove him crazy*
> *And then it drove him sane.*

Through deepening our spirituality we will restore a withering and destructive culture and gain access to the psychic energy necessary to take our place as peacemakers in today's world – people like Dante, who ascended from the Inferno to freedom, and Richard Price, who achieved wholeness after facing his pain.

When we join our participation in what Br. David Steindl-Rast OSB calls "the second superpower," we will begin to realize a growing movement for peace. This peace will be

- More than a truce: it is love and forgiveness, and recognizes that the price of every gun is a theft from the poor.

- Saying yes to reverence, dialogue and sensitivity, and saying yes to economic and educational security and affordable housing security.

- Saying no to violence, competition and war, and saying no to the terrorism of poverty, ignorance, homelessness, racism, imperialism and ecological devastation.

yes to mercy, kindness, forgiveness, cooperation and rgence of the heart, whereby we summon the courage up for freedom and take back our country, heal all ___ion, celebrate the sheer joy of living, and realize that there will be no peace on earth until there is peace with Earth.

- Saying yes to a peace that will give birth to a culture rooted in a new religious sensitivity and as a second superpower for the planet.

Together we can forge

- A culture of confidence and depth
- A culture of compassion and admiration
- A culture of beauty and identity for each participant
- A culture of concern and reciprocity
- A culture of creativity and engagement
- A culture of gratitude and collaboration
- A culture of struggle and fulfillment
- A culture of challenge and change
- A culture of action and reflection
- A culture of story and deep listening
- A culture of justice and reverence for the voiceless
- A culture of flexibility and focus
- A culture of transcendence and transformation
- A culture of tenderness and strength
- A culture of intimacy and contemplation
- A culture of amazement and mutuality
- A culture of listening and recognition
- A culture of mysticism and engagement.

Homeward to Peace

Let the beauty we love be what we do. There are hundreds of ways to kneel and kiss the ground.

—Rumi

We awaken, as if for the first time, to the world as primary sacrament. To a world of cosmology, ecology, community and wisdom. To a world of reciprocity, gratefulness and awe. To a world of cosmic common vision, creativity and reverence. To a world of natural beauty, mysticism, and opportunity for the Great Work, and integral presence. To a world that is holistic, that sees with new eyes the divine goodness everywhere. To a world where we *witness* and therefore *become*. To a world of gratitude for "good companions on the way." To the awakening of a hunger for hope that resides in the hearts of the young. To a new world that we can call home, a vision that will energize the next generation so that we can become a place of gratitude and glory for all that has been, is and will be.

It is this new world that will heal our hearts and minds as we go to the edge of our longing. It is this new world that will respond to the unspoken hunger for sacredness and depth. It is this new world that will give birth to a new genesis, a new moment of grace, a new Paschal moment.

This new world brings a sense of destiny founded on a sustainable future where peace with Earth makes possible peace on Earth in a simultaneous embrace – a peace that is possible through an enduring journey of courage, joy, celebration and ecstasy. Only then can we truly say that we are turning enthusiastically for home: home to our soul, home to life, home to Earth and home to the Divine.

Reflections at the Edge of Life

Thoughts on Relatedness

The New Story of the universe states that we all come from a common origin. We're related to everything that is, at one with all creation. This universe of which we are a part runs on three principles, which I call derivatives of a living cosmology. First, there's nothing created that's repetitive – no two things are the same (differentiation). Second, everything is related to everything else (communion). And third, each dimension, whether it's a stone, a cat, a tree or a human, has an identity that's uniquely its own (interiority). The heart of a cosmological ethic resides within the practice of these three principles. There's no racism, there's no sexism, there's no classism, because we celebrate difference rather than see it as a problem. The universe teaches us that we're not separated, we're in relationship together. Community is necessary for our very survival, as is respect for the uniqueness of each expression of creation.

Trembling

Unable to transform ...
Despair, powerlessness, early death,
unlived life, desecrated beauty,
alienation, suffering and pain.

Tremble at the doorway of ...
Joy, generosity, stories, presence
and communion.

And celebrate with newfound freedom
the "on the spot compassion" of
energetic hope.

Reimaging Life

Do not depend on the hope of results. Start more and more to concentrate
not on the results but on the value, the rightness, the truth of the work itself...
in the end it is the value of personal relationships that saves everything.

—Thomas Merton

I have always been uncomfortable with the presumed split of "change yourself, then change the world." It is more true to say, "When we change our consciousness it is inevitable that we also change our actions in the world."

The world today is one of unregulated markets, where there is a widening gap between the rich and the poor, where the ecological consequences of our destructive behaviour are increasingly visible and felt, where the longings of life are unsatisfactorily responded to by the ashes of consumerism and entertainment, and where fear and the tendency toward a rigid fundamentalism impede our capacity to be open to new challenges and the evolution of thought. It is new thought, new consciousness, that allows us to confront the violence and emptiness of our culture and achieve a critical awareness of the multiple oppressions that impinge on our lives and the life of the planet.

Within the depths of our longing for life is the desire for a new humanity, new ways to care for one another, to celebrate difference of culture, gender, race and class, to appreciate beauty, and to live simply with healthy food and clean water on this beautiful planet.

Our new humanity will discover that to care for the Earth is not just another "issue." We will realize the need to reverse the trends that are extinguishing the life of species. The new human will confront hierarchical dualism that divides spirit from matter, in which a "rank and split" approach rates pebbles, peaches, poodles, people, angels and God in order of value. This same value system relates women to matter and men to spirit, and thereby perpetuates a system of oppression in our institutional life. This system also justifies the plundering of the planet, and by using the language of rape reveals the link between the oppression of women and the destruction of the Earth.

The new human will foster a paradigm of kinship, with all species viewed as neighbours in the community of life. This shift will be accompanied by letting go of the concept of a masculine God who is understood as transcendent, remote and unaffected by the pain of the planet. Alternatively we will embrace the divine Spirit as the feminine face of God, the source that sustains and guides us, knits us together into a single community of life to renew the face of the Earth.

The new human will foster a liberating compassion that energizes all things and is in every way on the side of life. As Sr. Helen Prejean, whose book *Dead Man Walking* has become a movie and now an opera, suggests, we need to recognize that not only the incarcerated but also the health care system, people living in poverty, and Earth itself, are on Death Row.

As we imagine what it means to be the new human in a continually unfolding universe, we will be called to locate ourselves within a cosmological context and discover the presence of the divine in supernova explosions and the cycles of life.

We will be called to activate a cosmological imagination. Through symbol, intuition and archetype we will gain access to the consciousness of the universe that contains an all-prevailing energy enveloped in emotion, spirit and love.

The new human will engage in profound shifts of perception and action. Included in these changes will be movement:

- from individualism and competition to community and cooperation;

- from anthropocentrism (the human sees mind, pain and pleasure focused only on the human) to a creation-centred awareness that celebrates sacredness and divine presence in all of life;

- from religious sectarianism to a deep ecumenism with a renewed commitment for one's own tradition accompanied by an openness to the wisdom of others;

- from a divided nationalism to a true patriotism that embraces international co-operation among all "united" nations; and

- from a narrow self-interest to a politics where sovereignty is vested locally, to a decentralized economic system, to a preferential option for earth as the best and most benign possibility for planetary peace.

As the new human goes to the edge of her longings, our challenge will be to ignite the imagination, mine our heritage and participate, through new and ecological ways, in the democratic process, the education of others and the practice of "green economics."

As we swim like salmon against the stream of the dominant culture, we realize that the ideas and programs that flow from our imaginations have unique lives of their own. We see that creativity happens when we are willing to engage opposites, to see that when differences are honoured newness happens, as the union of a woman and a man creates a child. The creation of new life also occurs when the inner life encounters what is outside itself – when the personal and the communal become one. We will contribute to a more gracious and challenging world from the interactions of these apparent opposites.

The interaction between change and continuity will make possible the appearance of something new. It will be nurtured by deep listening to avoid the collision of "intercepting dialogues" (which occur when each person is planning their response as the other is speaking and so is not really listening) while making room for "the unexpected to emerge." "The unexpected" in this case is a new culture where divine energy moves freely in people's hearts – a greening spirituality (Hildegard of Bingen) that confronts injustice and retains a radical trust in a future not yet realized.

The new human will be energized by a fresh hope that summons us forward – a new-found courage to participate fully in the creation of a new culture where the poetry of beauty and brokenness will find its realization in a "sonnet of justice," a "song of compassion" that resonates from the heart of the universe and the divine imagination.

> Communities of memory carry a context of meaning that can allow us to connect with our aspirations for ourselves and those closest to us with the aspirations of a larger whole.
>
> —Robert Bellah

Bioregions: A Compass for the Journey

> Areas of the earth established on a functional community basis, that is, generally self-sustaining regions with mutually supporting life systems.
>
> —Steve Dunn and Anne Lonergan

I've found it helpful to use the concept of *bioregion* to draw out the implications of our relationship with life and with all creation. A bioregion is a self-contained dimension of the Earth, bounded by waterways, trees, hill lines – defined by the Earth itself. For example, I was born in the Great Lakes bioregion on the St. Clair River, which unites Lake Huron and Lake St. Clair.

A Context for Life

A bioregion is a complex structure made up of differentiated but mutually supportive life systems that are self-sustaining. There are some characteristics of a bioregion which are especially relevant to our understanding of how we are to relate to one another and to our environment.

A Context for Self-Propagation

The first such characteristic is *self-propagation*. If a bioregion is going to be healthy, every species has to have space to sustain life, to build its house so to speak. Same thing applies for the human community – we need enough space to be surrounded, room for both intimacy and contemplation. Living with others doesn't mean that you don't need and want privacy. Living alone doesn't mean that you don't need and want community. To receive what we need and long for we must understand the needs and wants of the creatures with whom we share the space and negotiate so that nothing and no one is left out.

A Context for Reciprocity

A bioregion is also *self-nourishing*. One of the great examples of the self-nourishing universe is the relationship between a mammal and a tree. A mammal exhales carbon dioxide and inhales oxygen while a tree inhales carbon dioxide and exhales oxygen. That's why we get into such a mess when we cut down the rainforest: our very ability to breathe is compromised. In the human community, we also need balance, both extroverts and introverts, people who can go off on their own for the day and others who need company. We need to respect our differences but also realize that there's a certain amount of reciprocity required. I think reciprocity is the human mode of self-nourishing. "I'll cultivate the potatoes because if they mature I'll have food for the winter." The universe operates like that. In this way entropy, the loss of energy within the system, is minimized.

A Context for Guidance

The third important characteristic of a bioregion is that it is *self-educating*. A few decades ago, people interested in growing spiritually had spiritual directors. In the old days, a spiritual director sometimes was thought to be the voice of God telling you what to do. I think the universe itself is our best spiritual director when we are able to engage in its rhythms in ways that evoke and create responses in ourselves. Our pets can be our spiritual directors. If you have a cat, the cat knows exactly what's going on with you. They come up to you if you're sad and leave you alone if you're angry. Pets are like that. So is the whole universe. We can learn so much from living interdependently with all of life while not reducing our spiritual journey's guidance to a human sitting in a chair across the room from us. Having a spiritual director can be a useful dimension; it's another mirror, but it's not the only one, and for some it's not the most liberating. To sit under a tree and write poetry could be a wonderful exercise in spiritual guidance. So could paying attention to our dreams and other ways of gaining access into our inmost selves and the divine creative energy in our lives.

A Context for Freedom

Fourth, bioregions are *self-governing*. One way to understand this is to realize that nobody's holding absolute power. Often humans interpret this to mean "Nobody knows what they're doing around here," and "The place seems disorganized." And then they immediately want to step in and exercise authority to get things under control. There is much to be learned, however, if instead of jumping in to make things run as we think they should, we step back and ask to be shown what is the most creative way we can participate in the life of the whole. This may be uncomfortable because, when we step outside oppressive structures, our own internalized oppression becomes evident: when we no longer project onto the system, we are able to free ourselves from what holds us back at a personal level. When this happens, our internal structure gets stronger; we feel held back, not by the system outside, but by the system that has been internalized. At that point liberation can take place.

A Context for Healing

This leads us into another dimension of bioregions: they are *self-healing*. The cosmology that we've inherited is very Freudian in its psychology. It says that there's a neurotic nugget in each of us, and when it's excised, we'll be free. The medical profession is similarly predisposed to operate and remove "the part," rather than return it to a harmonious relationship with the whole. If you look at how your body works, how the Earth works, however, it's self-healing. If you cut yourself, the body heals itself. This is equally true of the soul and psyche. What's needed is to stimulate the psyche so that healing can take place. It's not about analysis, about getting or giving advice. It is about getting the energy moving in your soul, in your psyche, in your total person, so that the woundedness that we have will heal as naturally as a cut finger. We need to be sensitive to each other so that healing can be maximized for everyone. We need to both respect each person's journey and challenge each other in a loving way. We need to respect and support this same self-healing in the plants, animals, minerals and bacteria with whom we share this planet so that a truly healthy ecosystem can emerge as a home for all of us.

A Context for Purpose

Bioregions are *self-emerging*. Materialist science says the universe is not going anywhere, there's no real intention to it, there's no real purpose, that life is meaningless. A bioregional model, however, says that there is an innate purpose to our lives, to a particular dimension of the Earth, and to our own journey. We're here to help each other discover our life purpose, our passion, what it is that really engages us as fully as possible, through which we can give our gift to others. Usually life changes happen when we awaken to the unexpected. Spirituality is about being attentive for the unexpected and responsive to it: it is about aligning our energies to the unfolding dynamics of the universe.

When we integrate these characteristics of bioregions into our lives – by self-propagating, self-nourishing, self-educating, self-healing and self-emerging – we respond to a deep longing to experience this planet as our home.

Celebrate

Pay homage to origins
Honour the cosmic womb

Be grateful for beauty
Remember your story.

Pay attention to this moment
Listen to your heart
Re-discover hope
Become what you were meant to be.

Embrace the crucible
Welcome the primordial furnace
Notice moments of the unexpected
Each an opportunity to
Celebrate,
Celebrate,
Celebrate.

Within this arch of wisdom
Relationships extend
Energizing commitment to a hope-filled life
Transcending all despair.

Wisdom Sources

If we are to live in a healthy relationship with the universe, we need to heed and honour the four sources of wisdom – women, indigenous people, classical traditions and science – which are repressed in our society. We don't hear women's voices the way we should; the indigenous people have been abused; classical traditions have retreated from relevance; and science has become materialism. But there is something to retrieve in all these wisdom sources.

We need to draw forth the voices that are not heard and celebrated. It is these voices that are most revelatory; because they are oppressed they are most authentically the voice of the divine.

The sense of inclusivity is the central contribution of women's wisdom and is absolutely counter to our patriarchal culture of hierarchical dualism. Body is connected to mind, Earth to person. Women's wisdom nurtures a dialectical and inclusive consciousness on all levels.

Indigenous people live in the universe; their lives express an integral presence to the community of life. The post-industrial society does not. One of the reasons we honour the indigenous peoples is that they remind us that we are embedded in the dynamics of life, that each of us has an indigenous wisdom in our own soul. The things we learn by studying culture and spirituality, they learned at their grandmother's knee.

Our classical traditions are a lot like our families. To be totally free, we need to come to terms with our roots. We can't just say, "that's not going to work." We're culturally coded into these traditions, and they have much more influence on us than we think. We need to retrieve the best of these traditions, particularly the mystical and prophetic dimensions, and reflect on them in the context of the universe itself.

Science reveals much about our spiritual journey. Through reflecting on evolution we discover that the great transformational moments of the universe have parallels in our lives.

The flaring forth of the original fireball reminds us of our own beginnings and the events that have taken place over time.

The formation of the earth invites us to ponder our connection to creation and the beauty that is ours to commune with.

The bursting forth of life on earth, the plants and animals, reminds us that we are deeply related to all the members of the earth community.

The birth of the human challenges each of us to assume our responsibility as a people to live in a more mutually enhancing way with Earth and every species.

Through integrating the characteristics of the bioregion, the wisdom of women, indigenous people, the mystical and prophetic roots of our traditions, and the principles of the universe into our lives, we deepen our relationship with creation and live with planet Earth in a more mutually enhancing way.

Liberation and Life – Action/Reflection

What encounters with people, and nature, have deepened your desire to ponder the meaning of freedom and existence? What holds you back from being fully present and engaging in a life of freedom and fulfillment for every species? How have these moments of intimacy nurtured your efforts to be an instrument of liberation for people and the planet? In what way has creativity deepened your capacity in the art of life?

Rediscovering Life

To plumb the mysterious depths of life we

- Plunge into the deepest recesses of the human heart and the heart of the universe.

- Play, pray, act, reflect, write, create, relate, dialogue, remain silent, and become newly aware of and connected to the person that we can become, and more fully realize the deeper purpose of our existence and calling.

- Become fully immersed in and critically aware of our toxic culture, yet not obsessed by it, so that we can learn to create clarity in our imagination and focus in our heart as we strive to "become delivered to our self" and transform toxicity into justice.

- Surrender to the wild energy of the cosmos whose power and potential take us to a new level of uncertainty and surprise, where the universe, activated by the divine creative energy, can do its work and we can do ours.

- Relax; don't "force the river" while creating the capacity to become fully focused and engaged, yet detached from the outcome.

- Be willing to ponder the possibility that the universe can become our teacher and template for a new vision of engagement and justice that can transcend and surpass previous approaches too often embedded in formats of domination and inversion rather than conversion, power over rather than power from within, division rather than inclusion.

"Cosmogenesis ends in a state of ultimate fulfillment, the culmination of the entire process where all things are gathered up in God."
—Leonardo Boff

3

Longing of Earth

Canticle to Earth

An integral and engaged spirituality that takes us to the edge of our longings for Earth and is responsive to interior and external challenges will include the following characteristics:

- The capacity to read the "signs of the times" in our toxic culture without becoming unduly obsessive so that our clarity is clouded and our hope in danger of despair.

- The practice of achieving the exquisite balance between an activism whose over-emphasis moves us away from our centre and a verbalism that, when out of balance, diminishes our engagement in the transformation of the world.

- The ability to discover, relate to and collaborate with people and projects whose world view and commitment are aligned with our own.

- The commitment to participate in nurturing a culture of hope and a healthy creation and in so doing dispel the tendencies toward despair and demonization that are rampant in our dominant culture.

- Provide access to fresh energy and a zest for life by engaging in unmediated mysticism through which we experience oneness with self, life, creation and the Divine.

- The dissolution of tendencies toward arrogance or isolation by nurturing the commonalities with our world views, our traditions, and our commitment to creation through our actions in the world.

- Periodic gatherings where we come together to break bread and tell stories, creating the opportunities for practices and partnerships of transformation that are innovative and aligned to our new and emerging world view.

- The creation of a balanced dynamic between tradition (continuity) and innovation (discontinuity) that ventures to the frontiers of reflection as we move beyond theology to an operative cosmology.

Longing of Earth/Creation

Let everything happen to you: beauty and terror.
Just keep going. No feeling is final.
Don't let yourself lose me.

—Rilke

Earth and Creation: Beyond the longing of soul and life resides a deeper hunger, a longing for intimacy, relationship and enchantment. A longing of Earth. A longing of every species to commune, interact and be admired. The Longing of Earth is engaged in through the revelatory moments that happen when we experience Earth through our senses. In sight, sound, touch and smell we listen to the language and longings of Creation.

Creation is a vast book written internally and externally that bears
God's signature ... it contains God's ongoing revelation and is most
deeply rooted and continuous manifestation of the sacred ... there
cannot be a contradiction between the book of the world and the book
of the scriptures... such a vision enables us to reclaim a theology of
creation ... they must extend to the cosmos theological claims that
have applied only to human beings but that are valid for the entire
universe, such as grace, final destiny, divinization, eternal life and the
reign of the Trinity.

—Leonardo Boff

Within the universe, the planet Earth with all its wonders is the place for the meeting of the divine and the human.

—Thomas Berry

Modern ecological movements have recovered the spirituality of earth renewal (i.e. creation) and married them to prophetic critique.

—Rosemary Radford Ruether

We each have a place, a role to play in God's community of life...Nothing is ever created in isolation from the rest of reality ...God's power to imbue meaning into the seemingly least of beings is coded directly into the process of creation.

—McGregor Smith

"We are faced with a planetary agenda of having to think about the well-being of the whole planet."

—Sallie McFague

Creation theology advocates a profound respect for the earth and for the created order, which it perceives as unequivocally the work and wonder of God, despite its pain, suffering and incongruities.

—Diarmuid O'Murchu

The communion of saints amplifies its scope to include other living creatures, ecosystems and the whole natural world itself.

—Elizabeth Johnson, CSJ

We stand at a crucial moment in Earth's history, a time when humanity must choose its future. As the world becomes increasingly interdependent and fragile, the future at once holds great peril and great promise.

—The Earth Charter

God writes the Gospel, not in the Bible alone, but on trees, flowers, clouds and stars.

—Martin Luther King, Jr.

Creation and Earth

Awareness, connectedness
Abiding beauty
Sacred mystery
Each a revelatory moment.

Moments of Sacredness and Depth

A Meandering

Beyond the longings of the soul and life resides a deep hunger within each member of the Earth community, a longing for intimacy, relationship and enchantment with Earth. Each species, with its particular gifts and desire to interact, invites admiration. At the very heart of each being resides the essence of its existence and the capacity to relate. The very Earth desires to commune with its individuated self, be it animal, vegetable or mineral. The reflections in this chapter are predicated on the conviction that the Earth is a seamless garment that encompasses both the social and ecological dimensions of life.

And in the silence of listening, you can know yourself in everyone.
Eventually you may be able to hear in everyone and
Beyond everyone the unseen singing softly to itself and you.

—Rachel Naomi Remen

The Planet – By Far the Most Important

And most of all, we North American privileged people who are
consuming many times our share at the table must find ways to
restructure our society, our nation and the world toward greater
equitability.

—Sallie McFague

We sat in the lodge of a retreat centre along the banks of the mighty Mississippi River. It is the site of a now-realized dream, The Oblate Ecological Initiative, a centre devoted to the development of earth-literacy and an organic garden functioning as a CSA (community-supported agriculture). In a room with spacious windows looking onto the river, the voice of Darrell filled the room. He was a man of seasoned years and profound commitment. He spoke of acts of justice and citizen diplomacy that were both frightening and inspiring to hear, such as a story of working among the poor in Brazil with Dom Hêlder Câmara. His moving narrative touched only briefly upon the highlights of his prophetic journey, and I felt moved to ask, "As a man so committed to a life of justice, how do you view the project of an Earth-Literacy Learning Center in relation to all that you have done and the issues that have captured your energy and your life?" Without hesitation he declared decisively, "This is by far the most important."

Later, we walked around the grounds and visited the newly planted organic garden, the site of a future CSA, and we gratefully acknowledged that the work of ecology and Earth-based spirituality are truly an authentic task for our generation. As we were shown around this garden, I reflected on our conversation with Darrell, this man of justice, and on the work of the Center, I realized at a new level that the work of Earth-literacy is truly a work of justice.

Earth-literacy is an adventure in reviving the ancient language of creation spoken by all life, a language we have disregarded in favour of that spoken only by humans. Creation itself, not any religion's scripture, is the primary vehicle of communication between the Divine and humanity. Within this garden I became aware that the process of cultivating, growing, harvesting, consuming and planting is a profound experience, not just for maintaining our health, but for attuning our lives to the dynamics of the universe and the processes of the Earth. As we concluded our visit I was grateful to find in Darrell's words an affirmation of my belief in the importance of communion with the Earth, and for the courage and initiative of Maurice Lange, whose task it was and is to direct this new work.

Later, as I contemplated the events of our day, I remembered and celebrated parallel projects taking place in different parts of the United States as well as in Ireland, Australia, New Zealand, Africa, Korea and Canada. Suddenly they seemed like lights illuminating the darkness of our cultural soul.

May God grant it to me always to hear,
and make others hear,
the music of all things so vividly
that we are swept away in its rapture.

—Teilhard de Chardin

The following was written later as a portion of the closing celebration of our Brothers of Earth gathering at Genesis Farm. Each of us was invited to compose an affirmation for one of the Brothers of the Earth; it was my good fortune to pick Darrell:

Darrell, you are a man of justice,
a teller of the new story,
a reinventer of the Oblate charism,
a person of compassion and courage,
an advocate and midwife of the Oblate Ecological Initiative,
a cosmological troubadour evoking the dream of the Earth
with people of faith throughout the land.

Darrell, I celebrate you and your place
in the Great Work — it's as you say,
By Far the Most Important.

A Village of Hope

Why can't your hopes be momentous as well? After a thousand years in which the human genius for technology has come at the expense of the planet,

you hope that that same genius can now heal nature,

protect the plethora of species,

and restore the Earth to her honoured place as mother.

—James Carroll

Earthaven is nestled in the mountains of North Carolina just outside the city of Asheville. Within this unassuming yet daring experiment, I saw glimpses of the world that our deepest longing call us to build. From the time I first heard of it, I had felt called to visit this experiment in living within the dynamics of the earth.

At Earthaven, men, women and children are discovering new ways to build homes, to access power and to gain a livelihood. They are totally off the commercial electric grid – their energy is solar, they grow their own food, they build their own homes. This shared activity affords them a space for both privacy and relationship, contemplation and intimacy. Earthaven is an intergenerational community whose goal is to live in a mutually enhancing manner with the land. Through courage, imagination and commitment, they dedicate their labour to sustainability.

One Sunday evening, I joined them in their community centre, a 13-sided building whose architecture reflects the Mayan solar calendar. There I met people who had followed their dreams to participate in this potential prototype for the future of our race. They have made a radical break with the consumerism of the dominant American culture and live a life of simplicity in order to build a better world for their children, where lifestyle does not come at the price of pollution or depletion of the Earth's finite resources. Following the introductions, we began our dialogue by relating the story of the universe and its transformations from the initial fireball to the galactic, earth, life and human periods in order to create a context in which to place the personal narratives of Earthaven and its creators. The responses were powerful, spontaneous and moving.

One of the early members told of the original formulation of the dream, the shattering of previous attempts, and how the group had finally secured the property on which Earthaven is being built. Subsequently, others chimed in about how they came to join this adventure and what brought them to this sacred place, now a beacon of hope and a growing manifestation of the "reinvention of humanity and culture" of which Thomas Berry so eloquently speaks.

As we listened to the stories of how people felt called to Earthaven, it seemed to me that they were "cultural canaries" driven from the toxicity of the outside world to form a sustainable community. One man told of riding his bicycle across the country to take a course in "permaculture" (permanent agriculture), only to remain and raise a family. Some spoke of searching for a way of life apart from the consumption-mad world. Others recounted their disenchantment with corporate America, and their deep desire to live intentionally. Some of the older people there announced that having raised their families, they were free to live in the manner they had always wished. As the stories continued, they were punctuated by laughter, spontaneous "aha"s, and moments of clarity. One could feel that the community centre was a place where the pathologies of pollution and social disintegration could be healed through the birth of a new vision.

As I listened, I recalled my years in personal therapy, as well as Thomas Berry's current call for the practice of a deep "cultural therapy." Therapy returns us to our origins, delivers us to ourselves, and makes it possible to begin again. It involves going back, layer by layer, to the earliest moments of existence, and then moving forward in fresh and unprecedented ways. Suddenly I knew why we were all there: Earthaven is becoming a laboratory for deep cultural therapy. With arduous effort, and great hope, people are fashioning an eco-village, a new way of living. They are literally beginning again. They are moving forward with new insights. With a sensitivity to the Earth, a new vision of lifestyle and livelihood emerges. They generate electricity with solar panels, and build straw-bale homes. Through biodynamic gardening, they grow their own food. The methods employed in each of these activities manifest a new way to live with health and wholeness on the Earth.

We had begun the evening by coming together in a circle singing the chant "If we're here for anything at all, it's to take care of the Earth!" As we dispersed at the end of the evening, the chant reverberated in my ears and I felt very connected to this noble experiment that challenges us to dream new dreams, imagine new lives.

Let the Earth and all its living creatures live their wild, fierce, serene and abundant life.

—Thomas Berry

Five Stations of Hope

The reflections that took place in our classroom became symbolic language for the eco-village described above.

As we entered the classroom that November evening, the question written on the board summed up the focus of the event: "What is your vision of a dynamic relationship between the New Story and the culture?" In other words, how can we contribute to the creation of a new culture based on our understanding of the new cosmology?

The ritual prepared by the Sophia Center students was a profound response to the question. First, we were invited to process through an arch symbolizing a rite of passage into a context for a new consciousness and a new culture, a place of geo-justice and engaged cosmology.

Once present in this new space, we were invited to visit each of the five stations at our own pace. Although they were offered to us in no particular order, I felt there was an intrinsic logic to the process which I will follow in my description.

I visited the "Earth Station" first. Here, amid candles, cloth and statements about the Earth, we were invited to plant a seed in the moist soil provided and to water it. We then placed a paper cup containing the newly planted seed among the candles that illuminated the darkness of the room. This station I have named the "Vocation Station," the place where the seeds of our passion for the Earth can grow and flourish.

Next I moved to the "Wishing Well Station." Here we were invited to take a pebble from a tray and place it in a "wishing well" while making a wish for the Earth. My own wish, as I let go of the pebble, was that everyone present would be able to live in such a way that our wishes for the Earth could be realized. In turn I named this station "The Vision Station," feeling deeply that if our vocations and the call of the Earth were to be realized, if our seeds were going to grow, they would need to be supported and fostered by a vision strong and clear enough to make it possible.

From the Wishing Well I moved to the "Meditation Station." Here people were sitting on cushions or chairs around candles surrounded by quotations such as "Mysticism is the number one anchor for global solidarity" (David Steindl-Rast). As I joined the others at this station it became profoundly clear, once again, that a new, creative and just culture will only be realized when we who are committed to the task recognize that deep, consistent spiritual practices like sitting in meditation will be necessary. Only then will our vocations flourish and our dreams bear fruit. A "Meditation Station" is definitely integral to our task.

Next I was drawn to the "Poetry Station." Here we were invited to compose a poem and place it around a multi-coloured banner. I wrote:

> Cosmic origins
> Reveal the source of Life
> From which beauty flows.

As we responded to the invitation to create, I realized as if for the first time how significant is the imagination in the journey to justice-making. The culture that awaits us has no predetermined patterns or outcomes. If we are to realize our vocations and our visions, and continue our spiritual practice, it will always be necessary to liberate the imagination in order to create a culture of justice and peace.

At the final station, the "Action Station," I began to sign a petition to preserve our fragile planet and to write postcards to political leaders seeking their support. In doing so I realized that an engaged spirituality culminating in action is an essential component in the process of bringing about a dynamic relationship between our culture and our cosmology.

As the evening concluded, we were asked to gather around a large circle in the centre. This mandala, this symbolic image of the cosmos and Earth, represented also each of us. We placed our seeds, pebbles, prayers, poems, petitions and postcards in the mandala and created a community based on geo-justice and engaged cosmology. Each of us was present in the mandala, including the stations we had visited. As we savoured the energy present in the room, I felt more positive about the future and grateful to be among this dedicated and creative community of learners. I was grateful for the "Five Stations of Hope."

> *Liberation theologies make an initial contribution*
> *— they point to the intense connection between all forms of oppression,*
> *and especially between that of poor people and degraded nature.*

—Leonardo Boff

Always Nurturing

> *With gratitude for the freshness of the air*
> *The wisdom of the trees*
> *The hunger of the soul*
> *And acceptance of the divine, always*
> *inclusive and nurturing new life.*

Brothers of Earth

> *Go confidently in the direction of your dreams. Live the life you've imagined.*

—Henry David Thoreau

> *We need to move from a spirituality of alienation from the natural world to a spirituality of intimacy with the natural world, from a spirituality of the divine as revealed in verbal liberation to a spirituality of the divine as revealed in the visible world about us.*

—Thomas Berry

They came to North Carolina as Brothers of Earth to honour the vision and voice of Thomas Berry, an elder, geologian and wisdom figure who had inspired their lives and invited them to join their energies to the Great Work that is calling us into a more mutually enhancing relationship with Earth and every species. Brothers of Earth is a developing non-organization of men who are engaged in ecological spirituality and who gather for information, support and the possibility of common action. They represent a broad spectrum of careers and commitments and are drawn together by the impulse to restore the planet, restructure society and reenergize the spirit.

They came as a gathering of men: authors whose books had inspired others, former social workers who now dedicated their energies to the Earth, members of the Passionist community of which Thomas Berry is a member and whose personal prophetic efforts encouraged each of us on our journeys, lawyers and judges whose work toward justice was a powerful example in their communities, former government workers and intelligence people who now dedicate their considerable gifts to the work of justice for Earth and every species, a young priest whose vocation had been redirected by Berry's prophetic voice to the cause of Earth literacy and community-supported agriculture. They came as people on a journey following the insights of their current context, as a people with hearts aching for all that is being destroyed – sometimes confused about their role in what needs to be done, yet with an emerging flame of hope that the story of the universe is summoning us to take our place in fulfilling the historical mission to which each of us is called at this critical yet promising moment.

Brothers of Earth is a gathering of men of different callings, traditions and regions who are engaged in the spirituality of the Earth, a gathering that provides an important context for the Great Work we are called to do at this critical moment in Earth's history.

The Brothers of Earth come together to share stories, strengthen support systems and energize their spirit. In their gatherings they ponder the Story of the Universe and its implications for their lives; in their ponderings they realize anew that the tree, the bird and the river tell the story.

In their reflection on the New Story they pondered

- Intimacy with the natural world.
- Listening to the voice of creation.
- Moments of gratitude and praise.
- The integration of mind and body, religion and science, the personal and the planetary, personal journey and leadership in the Great Work.

Brothers of Earth is a response to all that is being destroyed on our beautiful planet. In our spiritual journey we move from alienation to intimacy, from verbal revelation to a universe perceived as the arena of divine disclosure, from empathy for human pathos to an increased awareness of and response to the ecological bereavement that is evoked by the devastation of the Earth.

The following reflection was composed to name this "moment of grace" in all our lives:

- There is a deep mystery involved that needs to be respected, celebrated and shared.

- Our vision evokes the possibility of an integral life (vision, cosmology and lifestyle) where the text and context of one's life can be holistic and one.

- The balance of being rooted in the tradition, yet moving forward with a new cosmological perspective, is a prophetic work.

- The vision of being members of a communion of subjects inclusive of all wisdom and all species is an energizing view.

- The willingness to live the question, be in the gap and allow the universe to guide the process is a courageous and compelling characteristic of our new venture.

- The organic nature of the process of being open to interaction is a sign of the courage and deep convictions that are at the heart of this adventure.

- Our work provides a wonderful possibility for the full incarnation of this ecozoic vision. In this way it can nourish and inspire those who are associated and provide guidance to others of us who are engaged in making possible the emergence of the ecozoic era.

- There was a conviction expressed that in this new age of anxiety many will be moved to become instruments of transformation for a culture that cries out for change.

In summary we hold a vision

- Of commitment and authenticity, where consciousness goes deep.

- Where there is a spontaneity of life, a greening of the soul.
- Of reciprocity, where energy goes in and comes out.
- Open to the future, evolving, never finished.
- That supports parallel projects, makes connections.
- Of deep Mystery, of Call and Vocation.
- With enough Mystery, Vision and Congruence to make it multi-valented and paradoxical.
- Within a functional cosmology.
- That is integral, mystical and engaged.
- Congruent at every level.
- That is not autistic or escapist.
- With a deep activism, a dream that empowers people to change the world.
- Where people of many lifestyles can come and find solace and support.
- Where people engage the Mystery and allow the Mystery to engage them.

We believe:

- We are held unconditionally in loving relationship.
- In an unfolding mystery that opens us to the sacred that is all embracing.
- Through creativity and listening we engage in the journey.

The art of living is always to make a good thing out of a bad thing.
—E.F. Schumacher

Realizing the Dream

In a presentation to the Sophia Center, Maurice Lange, founder of the Oblate Ecological Initiative, told the story of realizing his dream of an Ecological Learning Center and community-supported agriculture project; in so doing he described the elements of a dream. These guidelines are helpful as we reflect on the dreams of the

Brothers of Earth and develop the direction and purpose of our own visionary existence.

As we listened that evening we heard the words of Sister Miriam Therese MacGillis, OP, brought into the room: "To realize your dream requires vision, passion, and a willingness to work." The elements for realizing the dream were a further development of this statement:

- *Pay Attention:* Retrieve your early dreams as a child, for example, experiences that awakened a passion for life and remain with you today. Perhaps it was a time when a relative introduced you to the beauty of the natural world.

- *Honour Intuition:* Trust the deeper visceral knowing that is revealed when we focus on the wisdom that is available when we pay attention to our sacred impulses and inner promptings.

- *Let the Dream Evolve:* Let the deep desire, the longing, change and evolve. Our dream is guided more by a compass than a map; allow the deep longing to change the direction of our lives rather than become fixated on a predetermined goal.

- *Broaden Your Learning:* The dream will change when we widen the context and see the universe as the container for our journey. We understand our dream as an expression of the Dream of the Earth.

- *Live the Dream:* Realize the dream will require a practice. Be true to your deepest desire and make your actions as congruent as possible with the vision of how your life can be.

- *Find Good Companions on the Way:* To persevere and realize your dream will require that you have good companions on the way, fellow travellers with whom you can dream and act together. Offer and receive support as you journey forth in the realization of your dream.

- *Stay at It for the Long Haul:* To realize the dream will require prolonged engagement – the willingness to have a vision, passion and the willingness to work. As the poet Rilke says: "Just keep going. No feeling is final."

I Have a Dream

Without a dream, the people perish.

—Proverbs 29:18

During our inaugural gathering of the Brothers of Earth at the Campion Center near Boston, we generated the following dreams that continue to energize our work and prompt our efforts to contribute to a healthy and sustainable existence. As you read them, may they inspire your own dreams.

I have a dream.

- That I/we can be on intimate terms with all creation;
- That I/we can move out from our isolation into communion with all life;
- That fear of life will be overcome by risk and trust;
- That we can let go of our need to control, consume and possess, by allowing ourselves to be in the "here and now," and by accepting what is given;
- That we will learn to be intimate with ourselves so that we can be intimate with the cosmos.

I have a dream.

- That some day all the creatures of the Earth will live with such trust and harmony that we can speak each others' languages and dance together to the rhythm of the stars.
- That there will be no more tears and terror but laughter and peace in all the communities of life.
- That our rivers and oceans will sparkle like diamonds in the warmth of our sun, and that life in the water will sing the hymn of the Earth.
- That age will lead to wisdom, and wisdom beget tenderness and compassion.

I have a dream.

- That the days of wantonly destroying the air, water, soil, and all the species and inhabitants on Earth will stop and be replaced by a simple, generous balancing – of taking only what is needed for sustenance and sharing the surplus in compassion with those who do without.

- That the economic world and the living world will be mutually supportive and harmonious.

I have a dream.

- Of a garden ... East of Eden ... where men and women work because there is meaningful work to do, not just to get a pay cheque.

- Where children dig in the Earth, sail on the seas, wonder at the skies, and play with the birds and animals in the woods.

- Where adults take time to care for the young, nurture them, and teach them the wisdom of the Earth.

- Where the old live out their lives in dignity and wisdom as teachers, political leaders, guardians, storytellers, travellers and wise investors of wealth.

- Where human communities nestle into the landscape.

- Where the wild is still allowed to be.

I have a dream.

- That my grandchildren are embraced by an empowering educational system which will nurture their individuality, support their creativity, foster their natural tolerance and quicken their curiosity.

I have a dream.

- That every child will have the grace of playing in the ocean, on the beach and in the grass.

- That every adolescent will be gifted with profound experiences of his/her Earth self and universe self.

- That the demon of nuclear waste and fission be exorcised from the land.
- That we can all walk in the sun, drink the water, and breathe the air without fear of diminishing our health.
- That these experiences be recognized as our birthright.
- That Earth be seen not as an obstacle on the way to soul, but as the way!

I have a dream.

- That human health care is converted from a system dedicated to crisis intervention and disease control to a way of being informed by Earth-centred therapies, mutually enhancing for the human and the other-than-human alike.
- That we recognize in a practical and fundamental way that Earth is our primary healer. That through our encounter with ecotherapies to heal our physical bodies, we become aware of our ecological bodies, and dream to heal our relationship with the rest of creation.

I have a dream.

- That the practice of peace becomes prevalent in the world.
- That respect for diversity blossoms into overwhelming and creative processes for healing differences in the world.
- That cultural difference is celebrated and shared throughout the land.
- That we learn from the lessons of the universe, the Earth and all the inhabitants of nature.
- That continuous, lifelong learning and discovery becomes the norm throughout the world.
- That the religions of the world converge on a path of spiritual awakening and common purpose.
- That the resources of the world are distributed equitably to relieve unnecessary suffering and pain.

- That the young people of the world be invited into the centre of society so that their ideas, curiosity and energy can be utilized and respected .
- That all forms of intelligence and talent be recognized and respected as gifts of unique and equal value.
- That individual and community needs are respected, met and celebrated.

Great dreams are wells that never run dry.

—Michael Grasso

Imagine all the people sharing all the world ...

—John Lennon

On a summer morning
I sat down
On a hillside
To think about god...
Let us hope
It will always be like this
Each of us going on
In our inexplicable ways
Building our universe.

—Mary Oliver

Reflection at the Edge of Earth

Gratitude and Grace

The most beautiful experience we can have is the mysterious.

—Albert Einstein

Mary Whelan, an Irish author, community development worker, and founder of the Community Action Network in Dublin, declares that the basic characteristic needed in an animator for change is the cultivation of gratitude and grace. Gratitude is the capacity for heartfelt appreciation. Grateful people know in their hearts that what they have received is a gift. In fact, they approach life, whether the dawning of a new day, the love of a partner, the beauty of a lake or meadow, or the wonder of the imagination, with gratitude. For grateful people, partnerships and reciprocity are works of the heart. Modern community development is too often a mechanical process in which no one invests his or her heart. That can only produce a community lacking soul.

Mary Whelan and her colleagues are working to "ensoul" community development. Examples of their efforts include an extended ritual on the Four Paths of Creation/Spirituality (awe, letting go, creativity and transformation); gatherings to reflect on themes of hope, anger, and the history, theory and practice of community development; soul days on the Cosmic Walk and the Five Elements (fire, water, earth, minerals and nature); programs focusing on developing "soul eyes" – walking around neighbourhoods, noticing and retrieving such things as autumn leaves or syringes, and then returning to the centre to reflect together on what has been seen through soul eyes. By such efforts soul work has begun to find a home in community development; city planners and the poor and unemployed whom they seek to house can benefit from a shared inner journey and begin to work together as partners.

Soul work is becoming the vehicle whereby we connect the deepest aspiration of the psyche with the concrete requirements of a just life. We learn to make connections with the deeper movement of the spirit and the passion for equality and justice. Through soul work and community development, we nourish the spirit and make every effort to reinvent our attitudes and approaches. We replace revolution with evolution, dominance with co-operation, linearity with inclusion, and words with images, movement and sound. We resolve once again to move forward with the work of justice and equality in the world.

In October of 2000, at the end of my visit in Ireland, I composed the following poem in honour of "The Shimmering Well by the Sea," the home of Mary Whalen in County Mayo, Ireland, where she and her colleagues gather to do soul work.

More than a collection of lumber and stone
More than a place to live
More than a hearth and a symbol of home
Is the shimmering well by the sea.

More than a beautiful building now in place
More than a dream now come true
More than a context to gather and talk
Is the shimmering well by the sea.

More than a home for the restless heart
More than a project for peace
More than haven to heal the soul
Is the shimmering well by the sea.

More than a place to be equal and just
More than a place to be free
More than a place for the integral life
Is the shimmering well by the sea.

More than a place to listen and learn
More than a place to just be
More than a place for beauty and balance
Is the shimmering well by the sea.

Yes it's a place for stories and dreams
A place of mystery for me
As we build for Earth souls of justice and peace
At the shimmering well by the sea.

Freedom in the Struggle

Worldly power, the power which forces its will upon others, even when applied ever so gently, could only produce something different from the total liberation and freedom that Jesus had in mind.

—Albert Nolan

Freedom, freedom is a hard-won thing.

—Old Trade Union song

I've always been proud of my Irish roots, my ancestral stories, of overcoming oppression and of a small country's magnificent contribution to the culture of the world. I am proud of the people whose poetry and wisdom have influenced many with their capacity for mystery, their inclusion of the imagination, and the relentless commitment to justice. It is these people who, during the Great Famine, died of hunger or were exiled from their homeland, while the fruits of their labours, which could have fed them, were exported by the British conquerors for profit. This is a story with many untold chapters. This narrative provides the landscape for much good work, particularly the effort to be liberated from foreign rule and religious persecution. Over the years this story has been punctuated by hunger strikes, car bombings, economic strife and irrational conflicts over land, politics and denominational differences.

Yet this cauldron of injustice has also brewed up the Community Action Network, a project for the poor and oppressed, committed to the dignity and freedom of women, homeless people, children, the addicted and the unemployed. Today these spiritual warriors gather to explore the deeper meanings of the struggle, to go to the edge of their longing, to engage in the soul work that strengthens *their* spirit and commitment to undertake the challenges that lie ahead.

A new generation of mystics and prophets of the Emerald Isle is being born, a people who have retained their capacity to incorporate the inspiration of Patrick, Bridget, poetry, politics, Christian stories and Druid myths into a rich mix of wisdom, wit and moral outrage. This new unified field of community development and soul work is beginning to heal the ravages of violence, drugs, unemployment and abuse that follow in the wake of global greed, with its disregard for the environment, women, the church, health care, housing, education and all other concerns besides profit.

This new wave of soul work, accompanied by symbol and song, music and silence, procession and aloneness, creativity and celebration, intimacy and engagement, weaves together a New Story for the narrative of the Irish history. This New Story involves remembering Irish origins, reflecting on the events of the past, and finding new roles and deeper meaning in community action. As they give fresh expression to the language of the soul, they take up the challenge to create justice and equality. As they reflect on their stories and the universe itself, they see magic in their work and the opportunity for a fuller life. The urge to contribute to the health of the planet is a legacy from their ancestors. This commitment to soul work provides access to sacredness and depth. With new energy, they engage the most significant concerns of their culture.

As I sat in the kitchen at the Community Action Network's office, a woman spoke for all of us when she said, "Our challenge is to integrate all of this – that is to say, the cosmology and the call to justice." She named well where we are today, people of two paradigms with shifting cosmologies, changing stories, striving to heal the separateness between the spirit and the street, vision and despair, ritual and rigidity, the wounded heart and a planet both beautiful and in pain. I have come to see the Community Action Network as a womb for what many of us have been longing for, a context where cosmology comes home to the street, where intuition and cognition meet, where justice and equality are extended to both people in poverty and the impoverished earth. The defenders of the poor who work for CAN, and those whom they serve, seek to drink deeply of dreams and aspirations at the edge of their longings. They satisfy their thirst through a genuine partnership in the creation of living communities. They savour a time to celebrate, finding freedom in the struggle, refreshed with gratitude and grace; this phenomenon has a unique manifestation in Central America, Argentina, Korea, New Zealand and in other places as well.

A Hymn to Creation

Poetry invites us into
        the fault-lines of our psyches.
We know again the place
        where finitude and infinity meet.
Where words of mystery envelop the landscape
        that lies deep within.

Poetry washes over us
As words, however lyrical
Announce once more
That they are the last resort for what
        lies deep within.

The New Story unfurls before us
Unleashing the divine imagination
Announcing the cosmological powers
that swirl through the universe
And become proclaimed with fresh comprehension
Of humanity's conscious self-awareness.

 Peacemaking brings cosmos back to earth
With renewed hope
We feel again the possibility of
        a beloved community
A place where peace can happen always
Where hope becomes our oxygen
A Source of breath
Where we can once again inspire each other
And aspire to a healed and healthy earth.

A place of energy and zest
Where we can grow our soul
Become instruments of promise
A people of planetary peace
A people who know
As if for the first time
That the universe is
Constitutive to all our traditions
And a sacred experience for openness and life.

Criticize the Moment

The following reflection was inspired by a talk given by Fr. Gustavo Gutierrez, a man widely known as the Father of Liberation Theology.

Remembrance

We remember
And make present
The little ones of God.

In our recollection
We proclaim
That poverty is not their destiny.

The denial of significance is:
A condition of injustice,
A doorway to death,
A challenge to courageously
"Go against the grain."

The past becomes present,
Life is transformed, we
Criticize the moment,
Engage in creative action,
Celebrate beauty,
Experience hope, and
Are healed in our longing
For unconditioned love.

The Call to Justice-Making

There are two ways we are drawn into the work of justice. The first is as the wounded healer, like one alcoholic staying sober by helping another alcoholic to sober up. When we're dislocated from our own pain, our own woundedness, we're empowered to heal others based on our own incompleteness. Jean Vanier, one of the great prophets of developmentally challenged people and the founder of the L'Arche community in France, celebrates the transparency of the handicapped person – as a place where God is present because there are no socialized defence mechanisms, untruths and double messages. It's childlike authenticity.

We also are drawn into justice by the deep joy that draws us passionately forward into our lives. It's our vocational destiny, our place in the Great Work of life, our generational task, our historical mission. We work for justice because we feel called in our souls to do so.

The Political Climate

With Thomas Berry I believe that in order to create a climate where justice reigns, we need to transform democracy into biocracy. In this system, everyone has a vote, including the sheep that stop the traffic in Connemara. We need to incorporate an awareness of the total planet in our decision-making process. The city of Malibu near Los Angeles has a bylaw that every time they make a new law, they have to consider the dolphin. Everyone has a voice. I would establish focus groups around the country to discover people who have noble purposes who really want to run for office, people like Lech Walensa, who came out of the solidarity movement in Poland or Luiz Inácio Lula da Silva, the leader of Brazil, who came from the labour movement. Let's have a Lech Walensa or a Lula run for president. We need to re-energize the political process by changing our consciousness.

The work of engaged cosmology challenges us to bring a new context to our work; based on the insights of political theologian Johannes Metz, I would say you can't do cosmology with your back to the poor people and the poor earth.

Blessed are you, mighty matter, irresistible march of evolution.
Reality ever newborn, you who by constantly shattering our mental categories
force us to go ever further and further in our pursuit of truth.

—Teilhard de Chardin

Cosmology and Our Traditions

In some way the shift we're involved in does involve the shattering Chardin writes of. I think we're in an in-between time. Thomas Aquinas took the Aristotelian cosmology and developed through his theology a reinterpretation, a re-languaging if you will, of the Christian message through the Aristotelian cosmology. We're now in a different cosmological era, but we haven't completed the theological reflection necessary to fully integrate these insights into our tradition. We live in "in-between" times; like people on a trapeze we have let go of one rope and hover over the net waiting for the next one to appear. I think the Christian story is even stronger in this new perspective. The New Story brings fresh energy and a zest for life that couldn't be achieved with the current categories because they are burdened with a cosmology that has gotten us into trouble – not just ecclesiastically but into trouble industrially, educationally, politically. I welcome the task.

In my book *Ponderings from the Precipice* I wrote "A Proclamation of Trust":

I believe in the gospel of life, that touches every aspect of our lives.

I believe that the divine presence permeates every moment.

I believe that all life is sacred.

I believe that we are summoned by the Gospel to a life of peace, prayer, compassion, and justice-making.

I believe the call to work for transformation is a special gift.

Diarmuid O'Murchu says religion as an organized structure has a historical limit but spiritualities endure. I think we're in the beginning of a meta-religious movement that we're going to co-create together, a movement that is emerging from the consciousness of the new cosmology. The forms of religious life, of parishes, of families, can be reinvented in a holistic and just way. I don't have the answer as to what the changes will look like, but I share the question. I truly feel that the Gospel was written in a book in words, but that there is a primary revelation of divine communication through Creation. As Thomas Aquinas said, we have two scriptures to read: the book of the Bible and the book of the natural world. We need to be exegetes of both, to understand what Isaiah says, what John says, what Matthew says, but also understand the birds, the flowers, the plants, your children, your students and the people you work with, because they are divine revelatory sources as well. I think we need to be called back to learn that language.

Jim Wallis is an evangelical Christian, very committed to justice, very political. He lives in the inner city of Washington, DC, and publishes a magazine called *Sojourners*. He wrote a book called *The*

Soul of Politics and another one on *Who Speaks for God?* These are some of his thoughts for justice-work:

> *Get out of the house more often. Start doing something. Throw away the old labels — it's values that matter. Change the culture, not just the government. Listen to the poor people and trust those closest to the problem. Find new allies and search for common ground. You can't do it alone: you have to find new partners. Get to the heart of the problem. The work is not easy. Changing the world should be fun. And changing the world is our spiritual task.*

The following poem was written by Oriah Mountain Dreamer, a woman originally from the United States, who lives in Toronto. The poem was inspired by David Whyte, who is a Welsh poet living in the northwest of America.

The Invitation

It doesn't interest me what you do for a living.
I want to know where you ache for
and if you dare to dream of your heart's longing.
It doesn't interest me how old you are.
I want to know if you risk looking like a fool for love,
for your dreams, for the adventure of being alive.
It doesn't interest me which planets are squaring your moon.
I want to know if you have touched the center of your own sorrow,
if you have been opened by life's betrayals or
have become shrivelled and closed from fear of further pain.
I want to know if you can sit with pain, mine or your own,
without moving to hide it or fade it or fix it.
I want to know if you can sit with joy, mine or your own,
if you can dance with wildness and let the ecstasy fill you
to the tips of your fingers and toes without cautioning us to be careful,
be realistic or to remember the limitation of being human.
It doesn't interest me if the story you're telling me is true.
I want to know if you can disappoint another to be true to yourself,
if you can bear the accusation of betrayal and not betray your own soul.
I want to know if you can be faithful and therefore be trustworthy.
I want to know if you can see beauty,

even when it's not pretty every day
and if you can source your life from God's presence.
I want to know if you can live with failure, yours or mine
and still stand on the edge of a lake and shout to the silver of the full
moon "YES!"
It doesn't interest me to know where you live or how much money you have.
I want to know if you can get up after the night of grief and despair,
weary and bruised to the bone, and do what needs to be done for the children.
It doesn't interest me who you are, how you came to be here.
I want to know if you will stand in the center of the fire with me and
not shrink back.
It doesn't interest me where or what or with whom you have studied.
I want to know what sustains you from the inside when all else falls away.
I want to know if you can be alone with yourself
and if you truly like the company you keep in the empty moments.

Toward an Ecology of Peace

There is only one human agenda in these exciting and challenging
times — to discover the appropriate role of our species
in the magnificent process of creation which began 15 billion years ago.

—Paula Gonzales

Throughout history, humanity has searched for a unifying focus that would provide a context to foster justice and peace for the entire community of life.

According to John Cobb, Jr., for its first thousand years in the West, Christianity provided such a focus. With the onset of the Reformation and subsequent Counter-Reformation, however, it was no longer capable of filling this role.

At the Council of Westphalia, the task of fashioning a unified culture was placed in the hands of the nation-states. As the nation-states understood their new role, once again the drive towards domination and competition ensued. An extreme example of this occurred with the rise of Nazism in Germany, culminating in World War II.

As the war ended it was no longer possible to look to the nation-state as the vehicle of global cohesion and peace. The task was passed to the economic community – with its focus on prosperity. In the United States this is often referred to as "the American Dream."

There is now clear evidence that the post-war economic initiatives are fragmentary. Around the country there is a growing unrest. A broad-based coalition of people from the churches, labour, environmental projects, women's groups, students and members of mainstream America are joining together to take action to stop the global economic injustice and the growing disparity between the rich and the poor, the North and the South.

Fuelled by the growing cultural impetus of Earth Day celebrations (20 million participants in 1970, 200 million in 1990, and 500 million in 2000), there is growing evidence of an emerging planetary spirituality. Perhaps this is the most benign and promising organizing principle to bring about justice, peace and integrity for the entire Earth community.

The age of nations is dead;

if we would not perish it is time to build the Earth.

—Pierre Teilhard de Chardin

Imagining Newness

Energy flows like molten lava
As the imagination erupts
And from this place of birth and possibility
A new creation is born.

The dream makes life possible, the heartbeat
The heart of the universe unfolds
As we begin to pulsate with all that's possible

Our world continues to unfold
And much that is new shows up.

Let there be light in the darkness
Peace in war
Sunshine at dawn
Wonder in day and reverence at dusk
Returning to an enduring peace.

The Way Ahead

As we look to the future with hope and envision the deepest fulfillment of the longing present in creation, we see a sense of place to gather, imagine, heal, commune, receive and extend hospitality; to reverence diversities of cultures and traditions; to enhance consciousness, increase awareness and honour earth. Here there is a place for children, a context for learning and earth literacy, for nurturing an evolving consciousness experienced in a kinaesthetic way. Relationships are grounded in friendship and shared paths of service and compassion.

In this emerging context, the vision is characterized by ecozoic councils, by networks of information, support and common action; acts of hospitality; and catalytic interactions that nurture experimentation, prophetic acts, deep wisdom, reciprocity, mutuality and the experience of belonging. Each project and person will receive support for their issue, passion or call.

This emerging process may be described in many ways, such as a garden, a web or a constellation. As a garden, each person or project is a flower – a unique expression of beauty and compassion, deeply rooted in our common earth. As a web, it is neither vertical nor horizontal, but non-hierarchical, transparent at the centre, and strong on the edges. As a constellation, it is part of the new cosmology and multi-centric, with every participating person and project residing at the centre of an emerging constellation of relationships. In each case, there is a home for those participating in an engaged cosmology, a place where they can find rest, refreshment and renewal.

Song for a New Creation

Where there are ruptures in creation,
We are aroused to peace.

Where there is disquietude,
We are invited to balance.

Where there is discord,
We are attuned to resonance.

In and through the pain of our wounded planet,
We are called to make our Easter with the Earth.

From collapse and devastation
We rediscover within the risen heart of the universe
Cosmic peace
Profound harmony
Deep balance
Compassionate resonance
Pentecost for the Earth and
Geo-Justice with the universe.

Creation and Earth – Action/Reflection

What experiences of the other-than-human world have shaped your senses of the sacred and influenced the trajectory of your life? How have the rhythms of each day, of the seasons with the anticipation of spring, the abundance of summer, the vulnerable beauty of autumn, and the waiting of winter animated your soul? How has your relationship with the natural world awakened in you a desire to care for the Earth? In what ways do you feel called to respond to the devastation of the Earth and resacralize creation? How do you feel moved to respond with courage and respect to the promise and possibility present in each expression of creation?

Rediscovering Earth

Become planetary citizens of harmony, balance and peace. People whose imaginations perceive a world of geo-justice and who hope for a better world for the children of every species. People who perceive the new cosmology as a studio for personal, cultural and ecological transformation and a research arena for discovering practices and approaches to mystical and engaged cosmology that

- Is congruent with the new cosmology
- Is aligned to a more mutually enhancing future
- Is deeply connected to the trajectory of our own story
- Finds expression and culminates in a culture of compassion.

Through a transformation of consciousness and a listening heart, locate yourself within the great drama of the universe and participate in creating a culture of hope embedded in the dynamics of the cosmos and its unfolding into life.

With a deepened understanding of Earth as a living organism, discover a context in which life can be lived in a more meaningful way, with a deepened sense of place, increased insight into wisdom traditions to create and redesign our work to advance ecological justice, planetary peace, and personal and social liberation.

4

Longing of the Divine

Canticle to the Divine

*I will rise, I will rise
In the lives of the people
I will rise.*

*In the lives of the people of this land
I will rise, I will rise.*

*With the resurgence of the Earth
We will rise, we will rise.*

*With the spirit of the Divine
We will rise, we will rise.*

*In the places of poverty,
In El Salvador's people,
In the heart of Guatemala,
There beats deep despair.*

*Beautiful lands, gardens of Eden,
Are nations of martyrs
Whose people are taking
The road to Golgotha.*

The rich have been taking
The fruits of their labour,
The work of their hands.

Never again, Guatemala!
Your bishop's decree,
The cry of the crucified,
People and planet.

Come down from the cross
Of the army's oppression,
The cross of injustice,
The cross of despair,

Of violent homes,
Of enduring illness,
Of wages too meagre,
Of forests turned wasteland.

Come down from the cross,
Let there be no more martyrs.

Let us rise, let us rise.
Sing a song of resurgence.
Welcome this Easter:
  Economic justice
  Planetary peace
  Rights for all creatures
  Wholeness of land,
  Of all God's creation.

Let there be a New Easter,
Fresh hope, celebration,
When Bishop Gerardi's
"Guatemala: Never Again"
Is sung as a hymn
Of joy and of longing,
Of paschal liberation
Everywhere, everywhere.

Longing of the Divine/Spectrum of Contemplation, Liberation and Creation

Deep within the heart of the universe resides a profound inclination to commune, to be at one with, to heal the great emptiness and abyss that reside in the enduring inclination for relationship and oneness, relationships that reside at the edge of soul, life and Earth and flow with the pulsating presence of the divine. A shimmering presence that mysteriously invites us into the depths of our longing for self, life, Earth and our God.

God speaks to each of us as he makes us
Then walks with us silently out of the night.

—Rilke

Longing of the Divine includes the perceptions of contemplative, liberation and creation theology. It provides the spiritual basis for nurturing a mystical and engaged cosmology.

A flourishing humanity on a thriving earth in an evolving universe,
all together filled with the glory of God ...Such is the theological
vision and praxis we are being called to in this crucial age of Earth's
distress.

—Elizabeth Johnston

We will be the conscience of the universe. And our body will be the
whole universe.... But first we must establish the kingdom, perfect
justice on earth.

—Ernesto Cardinale

Each of these spiritualities (i.e., contemplative, prophetic/liberation,
earth/creation) not only aver their distinct validity, but also
continually interact in new and creative ways.

The divine is seen as the matrix of life-giving energy that is in,
through, and under all things sustaining and renewing life.

—Rosemary Radford Ruether

God is inexhaustibly attainable in the totality of our actions.

—Pierre Teilhard de Chardin

The time for contemplation is the spring that feeds our action, and our action will be as deep as the spring... We need time for the spring to overflow into insightful and compassionate action.

—Thomas Merton

We need to integrate our relationships with God, with ourselves, with others and with the planet.

—Mary John Manazan

Hope is another word for God.

—Clarissa Pinkola Estes

Whanaungatanga ki te Atua, ki te Whenua, ki te Tangata.
(Right relationship with God, with Earth, with People.)

—Rangi Davis, Maori Teacher

Today we are being called to align our actions with the evolutionary urge and dynamics of the universe.

—Carmel Higgins

Allow yourself to be carried by the same power that turns acorns into trees, blossoms into apples, and microscopic dots into humans.

—Wayne Dyer

The seat of the soul is where the inner world and the other world meet.
—"Pollen and Fragments," translated by Charles E. Passage

Our heart is that center where we are one with ourselves, with all others and with God... A listening heart perceives meaning.

—Br. David Steindl-Rast, OSB

To be dead is to stop believing in the masterpiece we will begin tomorrow.

—Patrick Kavanaugh

Let every word be the fruit of action and reflection. Reflection alone without action is mere theory.... Action alone without reflection is being busy pointlessly.

—Don Hêlder Câmara

Radical hope impresses people to put the imprint of hope on personal relationships, social structures and ecological communities.

—Elizabeth Johnson, CSJ

Reflection: The Longing of the Divine provides the foundation for an engagement energized by the integration of cosmological and cultural perspectives; strategic responses to "Earth's distress" catalyzed by approaches that are based on story, sacrifice, sensitivity to children, communion and creative energy.

I experienced the longing of my own soul and knew the mystic within. I felt the longing of life and was giving myself in the solidarity of the anawim. I heard the longing of Earth and carried the dream within, but could not integrate ... The presentation 'Toward a Spectrum Theology' gathered the threads of my belongings and named them as one ... the longing of soul, life, earth, the divine – all coming from the same oneness – capable of being integrated, lived, celebrated through an engaged cosmology.

—Anne Campbell

The practice of a spectrum theology of contemplation, liberation and creation will include a new consciousness and a new literacy. This will involve

- A literacy of the heart: An awareness of one's intrapsychic depths, interiority and identity that extends to embrace the universe (contemplation).

- A literacy of society: a critical comprehension of social, cultural, political and economic dynamics that embraces also the other-than-human world (liberation).

- A literacy of Earth: A capacity to understand the functions of the cosmos and listen to the voices of the earth that is accompanied by moments of awe, wonder and mystery (creation).

This new literacy will enhance our visionary and prophetic ability to celebrate and transform our experience of soul, life and earth, resulting in a hope-filled future that views each moment as revelatory and an encounter with the divine.

Moments of Sacredness and Depth

Mystical prayer brings you into the deepest intimacy with the divine.

—John O'Donohue

Deep within the heart of the universe there is a profound inclination to commune, to be at one with, to heal the great emptiness and abyss that reside in the enduring desire for relationship and oneness. Relationships receive their vitality from within the deep recesses that reside at the edge of the soul, life, Earth and the divine origins of all that is.

Within these levels of existence lives the pulsating presence of the divine – a presence that hovers over all creation and permeates each particle. This presence draws us into the depths of our longing and evokes the wonder and awe that activate the spontaneity of the soul. As we follow the relentless invitation to create a new culture out of the fusion of cosmic consciousness and social forms, we discover our identity in relationship to each other, the planet and our god.

God speaks to each of us as he makes us,
Then walks with us silently out of the night.

—Rilke

A Mysterious Echo—Searching for the Divine

When in the Summer of 2001 Sr. Mary Pat Driscoll invited me to visit her and her colleagues at the Children's Village of the Community of Oscar Arnulfo Romero in El Salvador, I knew immediately that I would go. This certitude was prompted by an awareness of a deep longing I have felt in my heart and that has called forth the response that is outlined in these pages.

It is a process that began in my childhood when curiosity energized my efforts of self-discovery: a process that proceeded into the therapeutic revolution in pursuit of personal healing, and now finds its focus in the spiritual practice that invites me to remember, listen, let go, create and discover, through ritual and

140

storytelling, the deep connection between an awareness of the divine and the concrete realities of life.

The trip to El Salvador reopened my recollection of years of parish and community work and the cherished relationships that have shaped my journey, the people I have loved, and the projects and people whose joys and sorrows have provided hope and energized my longing for the divine.

At an early age I fell in love with Earth; I savoured her compassionate embrace and basked in the beauty of the St. Clair River, the stately maple in our backyard, the snow that gently carpeted our lawn each winter, and the leaves whose multicoloured beauty decorated our village each fall. More recently the longing for Earth has been activated by an awareness of the universe story and a fresh appreciation for the awe and wonder of the natural world.

In an even more profound way, Sr. Mary Pat's invitation resonated with a soul longing that has been with me all my life: the longing for the divine, the longing for God. Convinced that God is more present and palpable in the poor and the poor Earth, I journeyed to El Salvador. While there I recalled my childhood curiosity, and the memories of people I loved. I drank deeply of the beauty of this gorgeous land reflected in the face of a child, viewed in the ever-present portrait of Archbishop Romero, and that shines forth in the land. Everywhere I sensed the divine, the presence of God. It is this mysterious echo that I invite you to listen for, wherever you are, as you embark on this journey with me, of going to the edge of your longing in search of sacredness and depth.

Thoughts on Death

When death comes, I don't want to end up simply having visited the World.

—Mary Oliver

A three-year-old child waves out the window of an airplane, "Hi, Daddy!" He then turns to his mother and announces confidently, "My daddy is an angel. I'm talking to him!" He is the son of the professional football player who died suddenly on the practice field.

An elder was asked, "Where are you going to go when you die?" His wise response was, "I'm not going anywhere."

These two incidents fly in the face of the conventional wisdom that says, "When you are dead you're gone and you either go up (heaven) or down (the other place)."

You certainly don't stay here.

Death is an even greater mystery than illustrated by these examples. It is ominous and foreboding because our dominant culture is in deep denial that it even exists. Witness how we as a society participate in "the high cost of dying" with expensive caskets, prolonged wakes and cosmetics that elicit such responses as, "Doesn't he look natural?"

It is also true that we live in a "culture of death," a world where violence permeates the planet (e.g., Middle East, Ireland, Africa, Central America); there, life is cheap and death a daily occurrence.

Yet for many death remains a mystery, often feared and too little understood. Perhaps you have memories from your childhood when a pet died or a recollection from an Ash Wednesday ritual when you were reminded, "Remember you are dust and unto dust you will return" – experiences that only increased your confusion.

I suggest that the New Story has much to teach us; we are reminded that death is integral to existence. The cycles of the seasons, the way the seed dies so that a plant may grow, are powerful proclamations that deepen our comprehension of the mystery. From the perspective of the universe, death is a next chapter in your journey, a story of returning to your origins. It is a new chapter in your life, a transformation moment on the journey.

A friend illustrated this interconnectedness of death and rebirth when she said, "I was with my father when he died and my sister when she gave birth and the two experiences were mysteriously the same."

The story of death is that "life is changed, not ended." This lesson has been revealed to us from the beginning.

Through cosmological death the galaxies were born. Earth came into being and life flourished. From the perspective of the New Story death becomes a transformative moment when we are born into a new life, a mysterious transition into a new state of existence, a communion with the divine whereby we join the great cycle of existence. In this view, the angel in a child's mind and the elder's claim for his continuing presence make sense. Rather than an ominous ending to be feared, death becomes a threshold to new life, a threshold to resurrection. This poetic statement of Thomas Berry relates dawn and dark and captures the meaning of the cycle of life, death and rebirth.

> *This morning in the sky as the earth turns eastward, so instinctive the manner whereby humans and all living creatures face the glory of a transforming dawn; and in the evening bow to the mysteries of night.*
>
> —Thomas Berry

A Paschal Spirituality

"If they kill me, I will be resurrected in the Salvadoran people." Oscar Romero proclaimed these words with great courage and deep faith – words that have proven to be true in the wake of his martyrdom. El Salvador, his homeland, nestled in the equatorial heat of Central America, is an exodus country, on its way to liberation carried forth by the Easter energy prophesied by its bishop, who was killed by an assassin's bullet on March 24, 1980.

A divine mystery, a "risen presence," is palpable in El Salvador. It shines forth in the face of a child, the gentle greeting of a woman worn by years of poverty and hard labour, in the monument to the four women missionaries – Maura Clarke, Ita Ford, Dorothy Kazel and Jean Donovan – who gave their lives for their love of the poor, and in the memory of the six Jesuit martyrs whose bodies rest in the Chapel of Oscar Romero at the University of Central America.

Perhaps the narrative of this Paschal people is most present in COAR (Community of Oscar Arnulfo Romero), the children's village where his picture graces every room and his risen presence shines forth in the lives of the children housed there, many of whose parents have either fled to the mountains or fallen victim to assassins' bullets. At COAR, the classroom becomes an arena for liberation, where 730 students, 60 of whom live in the children's village, can overcome illiteracy and cross the threshold to independence, employment and accomplishment. At the clinic, upwards of 80 patients wait each morning to be received, metaphors for the deeply wounded soul of a country which seeks healing for the pain of poverty and political violence.

COAR is indeed a microcosm of a Paschal people longing for life, for belonging and love. Here the people of El Salvador have formed a village of belonging where they nurture a spirituality marked by courage and a longing for the freedom to respond to the challenges they face. The spirituality being born in the minds and hearts of the Salvadoran people emerges from their resilient response to poverty and oppression, a resilience matched by the Earth's effort to rise above the pollution and ecological devastation which have left it, too, impoverished. This spirituality is born in the wake of the cross of cosmic crucifixion: toxic water and polluted food, earthquakes and floods, a consumer-driven economy that justifies an ideology of unprotected markets, a violent military regime, sweat-shop wages, and petroleum at any cost. How does a country, a culture, rise from the foot of their personal, social and ecological cross?

Yet in the hills of El Salvador, the hills of Oakland, and in many other places around the world, something new is being born. From the hearts of the poor, and the landscape of the poor Earth, a cosmic Paschal moment has risen in our midst. A burgeoning spirituality is rising from the story of soul retrieval, of bringing the soul of a people and a culture back to life. It is a story of reversing the mechanistic materialism that has reduced the Earth to dirt and the people to machines. It is a New Story of reclaiming, a story of fresh appreciation for the beauty of a landscape: a story celebrated in songs, poetry and music. It is a story of vitality and depth, of bringing back the soul of the cosmos: a story of divine presence and a new-found freedom for communities everywhere.

This new spirituality being born today is unprecedented in human history. It is a spirituality of longing, energized by the determination of a people and the impulse of the planet to discover new freedom and new psychic depths. With this fresh perspective we are learning to live in an organic, unfolding world. We are learning that the dynamics of destruction and creation are woven into the very fabric of existence. This emerging spirituality is the spirituality of the planet itself; it is becoming increasingly the sign of a new Paschal moment, of hope for the world.

In this new Easter epoch, we are experiencing a spirituality of longing for life, a spirituality that hears the cry of the poor and sees in the raped rain forest, the abused spouse and the abandoned child a sacrament, a special presence of God. It is a spirituality that perceives the cross in offshore drilling for oil, the denial of rights to a river, the murder of Guatemalan Bishop Juan. It is a spirituality that calls out for justice to heal the wounded soul of a people, and the violence perpetrated against the earth.

Easter Again

The sun peeks out
And rises in the East
As the ocean becomes the empty tomb
From which our Easter flows.

Alleluias ripple on the beach
As huddled pilgrims meet the morning
And celebrate a breath of newness
That resonates across the Eastern sky.

It's Easter again
Resurrection happens
Hope has transcended all despair
And we are, once again, radically alive.

The Cry for a New Creation

The poetry of Earth is never dead.

—John Keats

As we answer the call to justice, we realize that we are a people with shifting cosmologies, changing stories, striving to heal the separateness between the spirit and the street, the crayon and crack cocaine, vision and despair, this magnificent planet and our inadequate theologies. As I journey through this time, I find that it helps me to keep my bearings if I look at the process through the lens of the Incarnation.

For me, the Incarnation is not just an event that happened two thousand years ago, as it certainly did. It is the ongoing outburst of life that we see when the sun comes up in the morning, when the flower blooms, when the child is born, when an idea emerges in our imagination, or when instinct or impulse calls people together. These are all incarnational moments, a time in which the living God is made visible among us.

With this perspective, the Cross can be understood beyond the historical Good Friday, within the cosmic crucifixion reside the Gethsemane moments of a wasted life, of enduring poverty, of depleted resources, of an extractive economy, of a politics ruled by greed and special interests, of a despair that permeates the soul of our youth, of the hunger for meaning that resides within all our hearts.

So too the Resurrection, our Easter, becomes an ongoing event. It happens when we become one with our God, with our loved ones, and with our Earth. It happens through moments of surprise, in times of prayer when we move from illusion to reality. When we realize that prayer is not as much about petition or contrition as about celebration and praise, about aligning ourselves with the unfolding of life, rather than asking God to make the world the way we would like it to be. We make our Easter with the Earth not just at the spring equinox but when our lives and our gatherings create an experience of communion that is alive and full.

Pentecost transcends the historical event that happened 50 days after Easter and resulted in the birth of the Church. We celebrate a Planetary Pentecost that continues to happen among us – in the moments when all Creation experiences harmony, balance and peace, when the Earth community is involved in reciprocity and transformation. Pentecost happens when the creative energy of the divine permeates the natural world and animates the landscape of our souls; when we become one with God, with the planet, with ourselves and with each other; when verything is sacred and sacramental.

Our traditions tell us that we're to be engaged in a re-sacralization of life, a new Exodus moment, a new era, a Planetary Pentecost; when we view the planet as the body of the wounded and risen Christ, we celebrate both the struggle and the hope that will take us forward into the future. Henryk Skolimowski says, "Hope is the oxygen of the soul." Hope is experienced in the struggle, not in the victory. Hope is the conviction that tomorrow can be different from today.

There is an alignment between the biblical story of the Exodus and the moment we're living now. The New Story does not replace the Christian story; it ennobles it, empowers it, and gives it greater depth, context and meaning. For me the Exodus is what Thomas Berry calls the movement from the Cenozoic era into the post-industrial Ecozoic era, a more mutually enhancing context for life. The transition from a time of Earth destruction to a time when humanity has a new role to play is unprecedented in history. We now have responsibility for the viability of this planet.

The Role of Mysticism

This new understanding of the place we humans fill in the web of life requires that we become emgaged mystics. Mysticism is a unitive experience. One of the things about past religious practices is that they've often taught us morality without mysticism. We've been told what rules to keep but have not been encouraged to experience the divine in order to energize and nourish our souls. Without such experiences we lack the moral courage and critical consciousness that will empower us to do justice. Justice-making without mysticism becomes plodding. It's obligation without celebration. Thomas Berry encouraged us with these words:

> When overwhelmed by the magnitude of the task before us in our work for the human community or for the entire Earth community, we might look out over the fields to the blue expanse of the heavens, to the clouds in the sky, to the meadows in blue. We might listen to the mockingbird, observe the bee or butterfly in flight. The flowers bloom, the birds sing, the rivers flow to the sea. Those same powers

that give the sun its radiance and enable so many diverse life forms to fulfill their assigned tasks, those same powers support our work.

Mysticism is nourished by creation. If we were living on a lunar landscape, our souls would shrink, our spirituality would be diminished. The mystical tradition will nourish us for the journey that we have ahead. It is an unmediated relationship with God. It can happen in your room; it can happen in the park; it can happen in your kitchen; it can happen in your encounter with your spouse or children; it can happen in a personal way.

Poverty and the Divine Presence

The mystics talk about the notion of breakthrough. Breakthrough doesn't mean that God wasn't there before, and when you have a breakthrough, God shows up. Rather it means that you are open to the divine presence in a new way. Gustavo Gutierrez writes about this in his *Liberation Theology*: "When you take away the barriers, you can feel God's presence most fully." Poverty indicates the presence of the divine. Gutierrez asserts that God is more present in the poor, not because they are better, but because they are poor. This is not a justification for poverty. There are reasons for poverty. There are economic structures that create poverty by their very nature, and there are systems to relieve poverty that in some ways are exploitative themselves. This awareness of the divine presence is in no way a reason not to work for justice and the eradication of poverty.

Reflection at the Edge of the Divine

Beyond Theology to Cosmology

The primary manifestation of the divine is in the cosmological order .

—Thomas Berry

In my apartment in Berkeley, California, a book lies on my shelf whose title has prompted this reflection; written by Otto Rank, it is called *Beyond Psychology*. Rank is one of the giants of the psychology world; originally a close colleague of Sigmund Freud, Rank parted with him after becoming convinced there was a new starting point, a new context for his work in psychology.

While Freud proposed that humanity entered the world as *tabula rasa* and that the work of healing the soul began after birth, Rank believed that the perinatal process – the experience before, during and immediately after birth – was powerfully significant and must be included and considered in the therapeutic process. In fact, he was one of the original people to enter the world of what is now known as "transpersonal psychology." This is the area where psychology moves into the arena of spirituality, where the practice of psychology and therapy can take us into the realm of mysticism, in fact beyond psychology.

In a parallel manner, I propose that the new cosmology emerging from a reflection on the evolutionary process of the universe can enable us to re-vision theology (the study of the divine). This proposal does not imply the denial of trust in divinity and its place in our lives. Rather it arises from the conviction that the universe is the primary context for revelation and therefore the appropriate place to engage in both the questions that give meaning and purpose to our lives, and the way we discover and discern the revelatory moments of divine/human communication.

As I reflect on the story of Otto Rank and his departure from the work of Sigmund Freud, I begin to understand in a new way the relationship between our Christian tradition and the New Story of the universe. Our starting point is that the cosmos is the primary context for divine disclosure; when viewed in this way our tradition is revitalized and becomes more relevant.

The focus of these reflections will be to discover, explore, experience and articulate a resonance between the passionate promptings of the heart of humanity and our relationship to soul, life and creation through the Genesis story, signs of the times, Earth literacy, social analysis, and theological reflection on our Christian tradition (operative theology). A mystical and engaged cosmology will be achieved when these components are understood within the ethical dynamics of the universe story as expressed in *Communion* (everything is related), *Differentiation* (no two things are the same), and *Interiority* (each expression of Creation has a unique identity and purpose). Following are descriptions of these components.

The Genesis Story: Master Narrative of the West

The Genesis Story of the Hebrew Bible is the master narrative of the West; its drama of loss and return to the garden has a profound influence on our psyches, our culture and our way of life.

We change farms into gardens, irrigate deserts more suitable for cactus to grow lawns. Our urge is driven by a desire to get back to the garden.

Theology has been shaped by this urge. Acts of acquisition and greed have been sanctioned as spiritual practices to enable us to get back to the garden.

A further extension is the doctrine of predestination popularly portrayed on bumper stickers as "He who dies with the most toys wins." We also know there is no correlation between the acquisition of wealth and possessions, and living a full and satisfied life.

The proposal of this book is that we need a New Story, a New Genesis: a story that is dynamic, interactive and relational; a story that dissolves anthropocentrism, individualism and greed; a story to enhance the work of partnership and justice, to eradicate systems of oppression; a story to nurture restoration and collaboration, which will focus our destiny, enliven our heart and be attentive to the voices of creation, liberation and contemplation.

Cultural Moment – The Signs of the Times

Cultural Moment

Each of us is born into a particular moment in history; our lives are profoundly impacted by the times in which we live. My life was affected by the civil rights movement, Vatican II, the Vietnam war, and the therapeutic revolution of the sixties and seventies. The pioneering efforts of Sr. Gail Worcello, CP, and Bernadette Bostwick, CP, to build an ecozoic monastery in the Green Mountains of Vermont, for example, grew out of an awareness of the new universe story. If this were the Middle Ages, their work would predictably have been education, health care or social work.

Our work is not only influenced by the cultural moment; we are also impacted by cosmological forces. Thomas Berry refers to this when he writes that humanity's historical mission is influenced by those "overarching movements that give shape and meaning to the larger destinies of the universe."

The Signs of the Times

During Vatican II, the great world-wide ecumenical event, a defining phrase was incorporated into the document on *The Church in the Modern World* (it is best known by two Latin words that appear in the first sentence: *Gaudium et Spes* [Joy and Hope]). That phrase was "the signs of the times." Attributed to Josef Cardinal Suenens and M.D. Chenu, OP, this phrase refers to the "expectations, longings and characteristics" of a particular cultural moment and the challenges that this moment presents. Reading the "signs of the times" involves understanding historical events as moments of divine communication. Through our reflection we gain insight into how to reformulate our tradition in response to the needs and expectations of the modern world, and to view each particular moment as an opportunity for transformation, in fact as a "moment of grace."

The New Cosmology – Earth Literacy

Our cosmology is our world view, our story. It responds to the key questions of our lives: "Where did I come from?" "Who am I?" and "Where am I going?" Through our cosmology we reflect on the origins and unfolding of the universe and our place within it. Properly understood and reflected on, our story makes possible an emotional, aesthetic and spiritual fulfillment; it weaves together an interconnected web of the universe, Earth, life and consciousness. Through Earth literacy we are able to recognize the Story and our place in it. This New Story will shed light on our tradition and energize our quest to discover our place and participation in the Great Work, the historical mission of humanity at this time.

When we begin to appreciate the new cosmology we become aware in a new way that the sound of the wind, the songs of the bird, the beauty of a flower, the mysteries of dawn and dusk are revelatory, and each a sacred moment of divine disclosure. When we remember our early years, and our early encounters with creation, we understand these experiences as a primary sacrament – sacred moments that contain the seeds of our calling and the context of our place in the Great Work.

When we liberate ourselves from the book-bound world, we feel empowered and discover more fully our identity and purpose. With symbol, gesture and sound we respond to the awesome beauty of creation and realize anew that we have become literate in the language of the Earth. Earth literacy becomes a moment of grace: a conscious experience of unity, an awakening to a deep presence of the sacred, an engagement with beauty, a threshold to divine mystery, to the language of Divinity that speaks of sacredness and soul.

Cosmologist Brian Swimme proposes that our moment is a time to discover the creative dynamics of the universe and become a mutually enhancing process.

The human being is that one capable of hearing the thundering galaxies and super novas,

as well as picking up the song of the bird in the forest, or the soft breathing of a newborn child, and a rising up to the creator spirit who calls all to the mystery of the divine, surrendering self to all beings. Everything is and can be sacramental.

—Leonardo Boff

Social Analysis

A mystical and engaged cosmology will also be nourished by our capacity to become literate in relation to the social dynamics of our lives; this is understood as "social analysis." The great cultural workers of our era were aware of the need to penetrate the mystification of society and see clearly the needs and responses required.

Saul Alinsky, the architect of community organization, was called the "Therapist of the Apathetic." He was convinced that we need to be able to penetrate our social reality, to move beyond seeing that either there is no problem, or that it is so overwhelming that we can't do anything about it. His work was directed at assisting people to recognize their powerlessness and begin to act with increased freedom, dignity and self-esteem.

Paulo Freire, the Brazilian prophet of popular education, was called the "Vagabond of the Obvious." His work focused on inculcating critical awareness so that people could understand the dynamics of their oppression and engage in acts of transformation. The practice of social analysis involves reflecting on the congruence and contradictions of how we see the world and its relationship to our practice in regard to society, ecology, culture and economics.

We can begin this exploration by reflecting on a commodity that you own (i.e., an article of clothing).

As you read the label explore the following questions:

- Who made it?
- Where was it produced?
- How was it distributed?
- Who made the profits?
- Who makes the decisions about its manufacture and marketing?

Social analysis can assist our movement toward a mystical and engaged cosmology by helping us examine what the product says about our lifestyle and our life. We achieve this by raising questions about society and seeking answers; it involves critical awareness and the work of justice.

An Operative Theology

A challenge for the believing community is to examine our Christian tradition in light of the universe story; this new perspective will be accomplished by examining our history.

Our Christian story begins with the book of Genesis; we read about the idyllic time in the Garden of Eden, a time of freedom and perfection. The story continues with Abraham, Sarah, Moses and the prophets; we read of chaos, the fall and the promise of a redeemer.

The New Testament recounts the Christ event; we recount the birth, life, death and resurrection of Jesus the Christ. The Christ events culminate in Pentecost and the coming of the Kingdom, the reign of God. The New Testament ends with the Book of Revelation, the Second Coming, when there is a return to the garden – a second moment of "idyllic presence and perfection."

The challenge before us today is to view this inherited tradition within a cosmological context: a context that includes chaos, violence and creativity. From the perspective of cosmology, suffering, death, age, destruction and creation are integral to existence; they are not to be redeemed from, but are rather to be embraced as the "bitter and burdensome" components of existence.

In my book *The Sacred Impulse*, I reflect on these theological themes. Within the context of the New Story we begin to see how our Christian roots can provide a fresh perspective on our spiritual journey. For example, we see that the Exodus of the Hebrew Bible is more than the liberation of a people through the Red Sea to the promised land. It is also a continuing event, an evolving process by which the human community and the other-than-human world participate in a Second Exodus, an on-going departure from the terminal phase of the geological/biological era of the Cenozoic to the emerging Ecozoic, that new time when humans will be present to creation in a more mutually enhancing way.

In a similar way, in the section "The Cry for a New Creation" I reflect on how the Paschal mystery of Jesus' incarnation, death and resurrection leading to Pentecost became a new story for our time, a great narrative whereby we see the incarnation in the birth of a flower, the dawn of a day, and the life of a child. The crucifixion becomes a cosmic event understood as the death of a rain forest, the poverty of a people, the devastation of the planet. Resurrection becomes the beginning of spring, the birth of a movement, the unleashing of an imagination, and the inception of a program about to unfold.

Central to the Christian story is the notion of the reign of God or the Kingdom: that moment when justice will reign on earth. From a cosmological perspective I envision a world of geo-justice and engaged cosmology, a time when harmony, balance and peace will be palpable and present on the planet. These theological reflections are intended to extend our reflection to embrace the dynamics of the universe and to celebrate our Christian tradition from a cosmological perspective, seeing each of these themes as a Moment of Grace, an opportunity for transformation and change.

Base communities in liberation theology and programs in field education have developed a process called *operative theology*. It is the movement from orthodoxy to orthopraxis. As children we were taught our catechism. It contained the credal statements that summarized our belief system; we learned the Ten Commandments, the seven Sacraments, and who God is.

Today we are being invited to describe and articulate the core beliefs of our tradition as our operative theology. In other words, what in all of our belief system motivates us to live "our gospel of life"? An operative theology asks the questions: "What are the deepest convictions, the visceral responses that guide my life and have their roots in my tradition?" Theological reflection provides increased insight into our tradition and reveals new possibilities for creative action in the world.

In *Life Abundant*, Sallie McFague writes her credo – a process that I would recommend for all of us. In this regard I recall a story told by René Fumoleau, OMI, an Oblate priest from France who, after completing his studies, was assigned to work with the Dene people in Canada's Northwest Territories. When he arrived he spent his first days in Yellowknife, NWT, conducting classes on all the major tenets of the faith; he wanted to share with his new community all that he had learned in his theological studies.

When he concluded his classes he posed a question to the people: "What of all that I have taught you is the most important aspect of the Christian faith?"

The answer came back. "Never lock your door!"

The operative theology of the Dene people was "hospitality." They knew that in the frigid cold of the North, the most important gesture that they can express to their neighbour was the opportunity of getting out of the cold.

In light of this story and your own, what is your operative theology?

What Do I Trust Is True?

Life begins with trust, openness, peace, acceptance.
Creation is about being held, beauty, change, tears, letting go,
homecoming.
Let it be. Connectedness is celebration, laughing out of control,
playing, dancing, storytelling, mutuality, abundant food. Say yes to
life, gratitude. Say yes to death. Say yes to mystery, to labour pains,
to new birth, to compassion.

A Mystical and Engaged Cosmology – Universe as Primary Revelation

The new cosmology reveals our present understanding of the universe, as unfolding in time and interconnected through a common origin. A functional cosmology supports a world of harmony, balance and peace, and is predicated on a world view that resonates with the dynamics of the unfolding universe. We could say that a "mystical and engaged cosmology" can be understood as an operative theology within the context of the universe.

In this way our theological reflection becomes meta-religious. It includes the wisdom that is available through other avenues of thought and reflection. A mystical and engaged cosmology will include

- Reading the signs of the times of this cultural moment
- Earth literacy and the new cosmology
- Social analysis and critical awareness
- Theological reflection and an operative theology
- Ethical principles of the universe.

Mystical and engaged cosmology will include an articulation of those spontaneous tendencies that spring forth from the human heart and find expression in a world view that is at once functional and a vehicle for justice.

Our approach to the experience and practice of an operative cosmology will include the following approaches:

- *Freedom:* The capacity and willingness to "think outside the box" and become liberated from any tendency toward internalized oppression.

- *Vision/Hope:* Hope is the "oxygen of the soul," the virtue of tomorrow. Children are the archetypes of hope and sacramental signs that tomorrow can be better than today.

- *Intuition:* The capacity to be open to surprise, to unleash our imagination, and embrace the moment of the unexpected will create the possibility of a functional world view.

- *Curiosity:* Curiosity will open us to events, insights and initiatives that shed light on our lives and open to the possibility of a new consciousness, letting go of the present awareness that holds us back and keeps in place a dysfunctional cosmology.

- *Initiative:* The capacity for creative action will be evoked by trusting the sacred impulse.

- *Transformative Action:* The ability to create a better world for the children. Through transformative action that is written in the stars and practised in the street is inscribed in the DNA of our soul.

Mystical and engaged cosmology become a moment of grace, a conscious experience of unity, an awakening to a deep presence of the sacred, an encounter with beauty, a threshold to divine mystery, a language of sacredness and soul.

Toward a Mystical and Engaged Cosmology

- Name your deepest concern. What most deeply touches your heart and calls you to work for a better world?

- Name the current cosmology. What are the characteristics of the current cosmology that hold the "dysfunction" in place?

- Who are the Prophets? Who are the prophetic voices of yesterday and today that you hear and read, whose voices are aligned to your own and speak to your heart?

- Roots of Your Tradition: Name your "operative theology" and indicate how it is the primary motivating force that guides your actions in the world, and finds its source in your deepest conviction.

- Your Personal Story: How does your story nurture or resist the advent of a fully functional cosmology? What practices of creativity and unselfconsciousness will liberate you from the oppressive elements of your story?

- Ethical Principles of the Universe: How do communion (compassion), differentiation (creativity) and interiority (transformation) contribute to the practice of a functional cosmology and support the alignment between consciousness (awareness) and conscience (actions in the world)?

In summary, a mystical and engaged cosmology connects the heart of humanity to the heart of the cosmos. It will nurture gestures of spontaneity and beauty manifest in the verdant forests, the azure waters, the song of the skylark, and the radiant glow of snow-capped mountains, along with clean water, nutritious food, healthy children, and a new soul for society populated by a new people who are discovering what it means to be human in an unfolding universe. This meta-religious experience will be a celebration of the realization that the primary manifestation of the divine is in the cosmological order.

In this way we begin to see that cultural moment, signs of the times, earth literacy, New Story, social analysis, theological reflection and the ethical principles embedded in the universe are contributing components of a mystical and engaged cosmology, culminating in a new ecozoic event, a meta-religious movement for our time.

An Engaged Cosmology

To be a revolutionary is to judge the world by its present state; by actual fact is the name of truth which does not yet exist (but is coming) and it is to do so because we believe this truth to be more genuine and more real than the reality which surrounds us.

—Jacques Ellul

Over the years I have been puzzled about how to connect the wisdom of the prophetic cultural workers of the past and the present with the New Story of the universe.

For some time now, I was convinced that the imagination and processes of those whose work I've known and studied were embedded in the paradigms of the past. In this way I experienced a dualism between my past efforts and current engagement in the new cosmology.

An initial step was the articulation of what I now call geo-justice. I viewed this as the process of taking up the personal and planetary challenge of weaving together into a unified tapestry, a seamless garment of social and ecological justice; this approach involves exploring the dynamics of the universe as manifest in the three principles of differentiation, communion and interiority; geo-Justice involves exploring these principles, and incarnating them in cultural form. This involves viewing differentiation as local, communion as global and interiority as psycho-social. Through applying the approaches of community organization and development and conscience-ization at the local level, I developed a deeper understanding of difference and its implication for the work of geo-justice as it relates to race, gender and class. Simultaneously the work of global education, the meaning of sovereignty of global citizenship as it impacts the meaning and practice of a human-world order, illuminated the cultural implications of communion. To explore the implications of interiority, I viewed it as the psycho-social component and found in the work of Carl Jung and Stan Grof ways to understand the "galaxies within" and that the psyche (interior life) is co-existent with the universe itself as it relates to body, mind and spirit.

As I looked to the Christian tradition, I explored the meaning of the three principles from a Trinitarian perspective.

In this way Differentiation as the source of uniqueness and difference becomes the Creator/God, more often known as the Father. Similarly Communion as the source of relationship and interconnectedness is understood as Spirit, commonly named as Holy Spirit. Interiority takes on the perspective as the source of the word, which we normally call the Son. I proposed that when these principles, now understood in Trinitarian form, become present, Divinity becomes palpable and present in our midst. Thus the work of geo-justice not only brings harmony, balance and peace to our planet, it also evokes and celebrates a deeper awareness and experience of God.

What remained to be understood in this approach was the worrisome awareness that the method implemented to translate the components of geo-justice into cultural form was still immersed in the Newtonian-Cartesian paradigm.

To translate geo-justice fully into the work of an engaged cosmology requires that we explore and make connections between the deep wisdom of the cultural workers of the past and present and the insights of the New Story.

This approach raises many questions; it also provides the opportunity to discover the deep cosmological connection present in the actual processes and approaches of cultural workers. This approach will heal any division between the focus of geo-justice and the practices involved in translating into cultural form the components of geo-justice, namely, differentiation (local-creator), communion (global-spirit), and interiority (psycho-social-word).

The work of engaged cosmology will weave together a connection between "the stars and the street," what is most prophetic in cultural transformation and the dynamics and power of an unfolding universe.

A Next Step

The vision of geo-justice and work of the new cosmology provide a fresh perspective by the practice of a preferential option for Earth. Understanding Earth as the seamless garment of human poverty and ecological devastation, we act with Earth in mind.

We are guided by the awareness that all our actions are guided by an awareness of Earth. When this is not the case, we are in danger of acting in such a way that our actions contribute to the oppression of the planet and the increased devastation of its people.

The Quest for an Engaged Cosmology

The reflections on the Genesis Story, reading the signs of the times, earth literacy, social analysis, operative theology and approaches to an operative cosmology and geo-justice mentioned above have led me to pursue an understanding of what I now call "engaged cosmology."

The questions now become, "How do we discover new and historical approaches to cultural transformation and the practice of geo-justice that will make balance, harmony and peace possible? How do we align our initiatives toward cultural transformation with the dynamics operative in the universe?" With this in mind, we will accomplish our actions without any separation between culture and the cosmos. The result will be a dynamic integration between the actions we undertake and the patterns in place in the universe itself. Every initiative, every action, every spirituality, and cosmology is contextual; they originate and flow from an awareness of both the universe and the cultural moment where the issues are personal, social and ecological.

Toward an Engaged Cosmology

With the cosmos as a next contact for spirituality we can address the challenges of our future. Engaged cosmology will include retrieving the eternal wisdom distilled from the cultural workers of the present and the past and aligning this legacy with the dynamics of an unfolding universe. From this perspective I celebrate the connection between the stars and the street and discover anew the possibility of an engaged cosmology.

Naming an Engaged Cosmology

At this moment of destruction and decline, we search for a new identity and ability to act. When we become consciously attuned to the dynamics of the universe and act in alignment with this awareness, we have begun to discover an engaged cosmology.

Engaged cosmology is an immersion into the deep creative powers of the universe and the most direct contact a human can have with the divine.

Engaged cosmology is a new context for our journey, a place for our longings where poet and politician are one, a cosmic journey of struggle and fulfillment.

Engaged cosmology is where we embrace intimacy and contemplation, communion and solitude, inwardness and prophetic action, impulse and practice, mystery and engagement, cultural work and cosmic consciousness.

The hunger for sacredness and depth resides in soul, life and Earth. This hunger is healed, responded to and nourished by an experience of the Divine as we participate in a mystical and engaged cosmology.

Engaged cosmology is a process and a pattern that finds expression in story, generosity and transcendence, children, interrelatedness, creative energy, magnanimity and liberation, self-healing and soul, originating energy and the sacred impulse, cosmic dynamics and geo-justice, consciousness and cultural genesis, the heart of the universe and a listening heart, interdependence and rootedness.

The strategic action of engaged cosmology will access the collective wisdom of cultural workers and bring them into alignment with the dynamics of the unfolding universe.

Humanity has the capacity to choose to act in a variety of ways (transgenetic coding).

When the initiative taken is based on our best understanding of cultural action and consciousness of the universe, it can be appropriately named Engaged Cosmology.

From the Stars to the Street

The starry sky is like a city by night... the stars like streets.
—Ernesto Cardinale

If we want to live happy lives we have to build into our daily life moments of vision and then let our action be formed by that vision.
—Br. David Steindl-Rast, OSB

The challenge of engaged cosmology is to make hidden connections, to bring together the stars and the street. This will involve bringing together in our awareness and our action the relationship between the stars and the street, to realize our role in these in-between times is to become hospice workers for structures and forms that need to die with dignity and become midwives for the new forms that need to be born. Like blades of grass that burst forth from the brittle and broken concrete that form our sidewalks and highways, we are challenged to break through the brittleness of a calcified culture and act in unprecedented ways, to become bridge builders to heal the separation between the world as it is and the world as we would like it to be: to connect the stars to the street.

As creators of "hidden connections," we become aware of the stark signs of a withering and destructive society and the second superpower that is emerging from the streets of Seattle, Washington, Prague, Detroit, Quebec City, and your town; like stars they illuminate a horizon of hope.

As prophetic voices of hidden connections we experience a fresh realization that our address for a life of accomplishment and fulfillment does not reside on Wall Street, Bay Street, Pennsylvania Avenue, 10 Downing Street or Parliament Hill, but rather at the intersection of mysticism and engagement. It is this address that will unite the stars to the street, and become the birthplace of an engaged cosmology. This is where our emerging awareness and prophetic action will become one act, an act of engaged cosmology that unites the stars to the street.

Following are five themes: Story/Narrative Cosmology; Generosity/Sacrifice Reciprocity; The Little Ones/Children; Interrelatedness/Communion; Creative Energy. I have selected excerpts primarily from the writings of cultural historian, geologian and cosmologist Thomas Berry, and the architect of community organization, Saul Alinsky, to illustrate the parallels present in their approaches to transformation and change.

Story: Narrative Cosmology

Origins are fascinating not only because they are so mysterious but because they are so important in understanding things. We explain things by telling their story — how they came into being and the changes that have taken place over the course of time, whether minutes or millennia. But the most significant moment in any mode of being is the origin moment, the time when it was not and then came into being. Once a thing is in existence, we can follow the transformations that take place as it passes through a sequence of events, either interior transformations or transformations due to exterior influence. This is especially true in explaining those profound formative influences that have shaped our sense of the sacred, for this is the ultimate narrative referent for our sense of reality and value. Out of this sense of the sacred we shape our life discipline, our norms of social behaviour, our explanation of life, how we relate to one another and to the wider world around us.

If you do not know the story, in a certain sense, you do not know yourself; you do not know anything.

—Thomas Berry

We have forgotten where we came from, we don't know where we are and we fear where we may be going. Afraid we turn from the glorious adventure of the pursuit of happiness to a pursuit of an illusionary security in an ordered, stratified, striped society ... When Americans can no longer see the stars, the times are tragic. We must believe that it is the darkness before the dawn of a beautiful new world. We will see it when we believe it.

—Saul Alinsky

Reflection

The work of an engaged cosmology will be enveloped in a membrane of story. We understand the universe and our place within it.

As we ponder the beginnings of the universe and the transformational events that have taken place over time, we discover who we are, experience a deeper moment of identity and destiny.

It is by knowing and reflecting on our own story within the context of the great cosmic unfolding that we will achieve a new self-awareness: an awareness that will provide stability in a sea of social chaos.

As we discover and tell our story and view it within the context of the Great Story, we will begin to see our role and place in the beautiful new world about to be born in our midst.

A world of wisdom gained by listening, difference without exile, and community without co-optation.

Generosity / Sacrifice / Reciprocity

All the great transition moments are sacrificial moments. Our present transition will not be accomplished without enormous sacrifice.

—Thomas Berry

For our ancestors a sacrificial act was a way of making holy, especially when the act had a bitter dimension to it ... individuals who act this way make clear a sacred dimension of existence.

The pervasive presence in the human world of both sacrifice and the honouring of those who sacrifice seems to indicate our awareness that suffering and destruction are intimately associated with existence itself.

The primal human insistence upon sacrifice can be understood as an early intuitive grasp of the reverenced truth in the second law of thermodynamics.

—Brian Swimme, Thomas Berry

The wondrous quality of man that from time to time flood over the natural dams of survival and selfishness ... these episodic transformations of the human spirit.

—Saul Alinsky

The teachers must die as teachers little by little, they cannot decree their own death, they can only be killed by the student little by little in the process.

—Paulo Freire

If you push a negative hard enough and deep enough, it breaks through into its counter side.

—Saul Alinsky

Just as hydrogen and oxygen need to let go of their identities in order to form water, so it is necessary that the diverse elements of the community be brought together so that they may comprise an appropriate constellation for the new community.

—Saul Alinsky

Reflection

An engaged cosmology will evoke and celebrate the enduring tendency and predisposition for the universe and humanity to engage in the dynamic process of self-transcendence. The universe reminds us of the generosity and the capacity to go beyond itself. The sun constantly gives of itself providing light and warmth to the planet; this expression of generosity is accompanied by moments of enormous sacrifice. The entire drama of the universe story is a reminder of the gift of self; the galaxies give birth to earth, hydrogen and oxygen surrender to make water. Creation and destruction are a constant cadence in the unfolding universe.

In a parallel way humanity from time to time embraces a "wondrous quality," goes beyond "survival and selfishness" and demonstrates "episodic transformations of the spirit."

These moments of sacrifice, so profoundly present in the cosmos, are also present when people participate in the work of personal, social and ecological transformation. In the educational adventure we are reminded that "the teachers must die as teachers" (Freire).

It is this quality of generosity and sacrifice that will be required to make the transition into a more just world. Generosity and sacrifice not only make possible a better world; it will be a world of beauty, a place where sacredness and divinity permeate each moment of existence.

The process of moving toward a more human world and healthy planet will include not only liberating the oppressed but also the oppressor; this process will include an awareness that the liberator contains elements of oppression and at the same time the oppressor is in some way a force for freedom.

The Little Ones / Children

Children need a story that will bring personal meaning together with the grandeur and meaning of the universe.

The child awakens to the universe ... It takes a universe to make a child both in outer form and inner spirit. It takes a universe to educate a child, a universe to fulfill a child ... So now we write our own verses, bringing the child and the universe into mutual fulfillment.

To deal effectively with the natural world, we must also deal with the human world, with the human world as integral to the natural world.

—Thomas Berry

The issue to be resolved is the creation of a world for the little people, a world where millions instead of a few can live in dignity, peace and security.

...To do something practical to help the poor, the hungry, the imprisoned and the powerless and a desperate search for identity.

—Saul Alinsky

Reflection

A constant preoccupation for an engaged cosmology will be to nurture, support and protect the little ones, those most endangered and abused. Every generation that knows its story, both personal and cosmic, will find its focus on the children and unborn of every species. The young need meaning and beauty to awaken to their place in life and the search for fulfillment. In our reflection on the place of the little ones we hear a clarion call for their dignity, identity, security and peace.

Interrelatedness / Communion

This sense of relatedness coming even before a first interaction, of a community reality at the base of being, characterizes even the earliest eras of the universe, even before the natural selection process of the natural world. At this level quantum inseparability governs activity that no two particles can be considered completely disconnected ever… The loss of relationship, with its consequent alienation, is a kind of supreme evil in the universe.

—Thomas Berry, Brian Swimme

The universe is a communion of subjects, not a collection of objects.

—Thomas Berry

We do not really know things in themselves in their objective reality, but rather by an intercommunion.

—Thomas Berry

The universe itself is the primary sacred community.

—Thomas Berry

There is a supreme mode of communion which exists within the human community, within the earth-human complex.

—Thomas Berry

One of the difficulties experienced by the human, one of the causes of our planetary, human and educational disarray, is that we have not adequately developed this capacity for communion.

—Thomas Berry

The prime illusion we must rid ourselves of is the conventional view in which things are seen as separate from their counterparts. Everything must be seen as the inevitable partner of its converse, light and darkness … and so with every component of the universe all are paired in the enormous Noah's Ark of Life.

—Saul Alinsky

It is this awakening of our people from the abysmal apathy that will awaken us to a sense of ourselves as members of the human family.

—Saul Alinsky

Reflection

A great lesson of the universe is that inseparability is a governing principle of life. We are born of the universe to commune with all creation.

Conscious that relatedness and community are the basis of our being, we joyfully realize that self-discovery is only fully possible when we enter into and experience community.

As we look to the stars we discover that the universe is a "sacred community" and our existence will be most fully understood when we are enveloped within a constellation of relationships. When we are present to each other in mutually enhancing ways, when we are present to each other in community, when we realize that we are all members of the Earth community and inevitable partners in an enormous "Noah's Ark of Life," we will then realize our identity as members of the human family.

This experience of being present to each other will strengthen us; we will realize anew that alienation, exile, loneliness and separation are products of a cultural pathology. With this in mind we realize that our desire for and tendency toward relationship with soul, life, Earth and God are supported and empowered by both our deepest intuitions and the universe itself.

Creative Energy

The purpose of this new energy was not to maintain the existing system but to change the system itself in its deepest meaning and the entire modality of its function.

With our new knowledge we can participate more fully in the emergent processes of the present and the shaping of the future.

We recognize it is the mythic vision that evokes the energies needed to sustain the human effort involved. The important thing is that the mythic vision leads to a sustainable context for the survival and continued evolution of the earth and its living forms.

This mystique must be associated with three basic commitments of our time: Commitment to the earth as irreversible process, to the ecological age as the only viable form of millennial ideal and to a sense of progress that includes the natural as well as the human world.

—Thomas Berry

The organizer is driven by a desire to create ... the passionate desire of all human beings to feel they have personally contributed to the creation and securing of any objective they desire.

We seek a world in which the worth of the individual is recognized...the creation of the kind of society when all potentialities could be realized: A world where people could live in dignity, security, happiness and peace...a world based on a morality of humankind.

There are no fixed chronological points or definite issues. The demands are always changing; the situation is fluid and ever shifting.

The human cry of the second revolution is one for meaning and purpose for life – a cause to live for and if need be to die for – this is literally the revolution of the soul.

All revolutionary values are primarily generated from spiritual values and considerations of justice, equality, peace and brotherhood [sic].

Complementarity – the interplay of seemingly con forces, or opposites, is the actual harmony of nature (e.g., yin/yang – dual powers, positive/negative, light/darkness, male/female).

—Saul Alinsky

Reflection

Creative energy is the source from which we can harness "the divine inclination" toward transformation and new life. It is this divine creative energy that will sustain us in our work to bring forth a world of harmony, balance and peace, a world that is mutually enhancing for people and the planet. An engaged cosmology will empower people to achieve their fondest desire for their lives and life on earth – a world marked by dignity, security, meaning, purpose, happiness and peace. A world that can best be marked by naming it as a "revolution of the soul."

A Synthesis

There is no compelling activity that is tied to the element of consciousness...humans did not simultaneously feel the demand for a complex and specific pattern of activity associated with each experience.

—Thomas Berry/Brian Swimme

Action that emerges from a synthesis of contemplative, liberation and creation spirituality understood within the context of the universe is constitutive of an engaged cosmology. An integral practice of dream, soul work and action is the necessary condition for prolonged participation in engaged cosmology.

Themes for an Engaged Cosmology

Engaged cosmology should mean taking action into the physical/ social world that is congruent with lessons from evolution and ecology.

—Richard Register

The following twelve themes were discovered through reflecting on the connections between the wisdom and practice of cultural workers of the past and present, and an awareness of the dynamics of an unfolding universe as described in the works on new cosmology.

Magnanimity and the Liberation of Creation

Engagement in deep cultural work nourishes a magnanimity of spirit. In the process we experience a felt-sense of oneness with the universe and all that is. Our engagement inspires a deep communion with humanity and the other-than-human world. We transcend narrow self-interest and are moved to grant each member of the Earth community the freedom to inhabit the planet and fulfill its role. We are inspired by the generosity demonstrated by the self-giving of the sun.

Self-Healing and the Soul

Prophetic cultural change contains a healing dimension: when properly supported and stimulated, both Earth and psyche demonstrate self-healing properties. In each case the cultural worker or cosmologist is more witness than agent.

Originating Energy and the Sacred Impulse

The process of cultural transformation finds its direction and energy in responding to the felt-sense of a sacred impulse that prompts our action, an impulse that we understand as the continuing expression of the originating energy that gave birth to the universe and continues to support our efforts and intuition.

Cosmic Dynamics and Geo-Justice

The harmony, balance and peace embedded in the universe find their cultural manifestation in the work of geo-justice. In this process beauty shines forth and divinity becomes palpable in our midst as we celebrate communion (global), differentiation (local) and interiority (psycho-social) in cultural form.

Consciousness and Culture

Engaged cosmology is an irreversible process that weaves together our cultural work with an awareness of the unfolding universe. We experience the support and interaction of consciousness and conscience. Our cosmological consciousness and our awareness of the world community create an integral presence; the result is that we act in accordance with what we see, and our cultural work evolves and unfolds in a manner to the evolving universe.

Creation, Destruction and the Dynamics of Rebirth

Cultural work involves the capacity to die to oneself and rise to the concern for the other. These deep dynamics of creation, destruction and rebirth are embedded in the process of life and in the dynamics of our traditions; they find expression in the epiphanies (Incarnation), Gethsemane moments (Cross), and inevitable outpouring of new life in the larger arc of existence (Resurrection).

Narrative and the Great Unfolding

A profound and appropriate approach to our cultural work is the practice of storytelling. Each story heard, told and celebrated is perceived as a paragraph in the great sacred story and a context that inevitably prompts us into action to resacralize our lives and the meaning of existence. Our stories, told within the context of the Great Story, create action to transform the world.

The Heart – Listening to the Universe

Deep listening is a practice that resonates in the recesses of the cultural worker. It is understood as an echo from the pulsating heart of the universe. Listening to the other and to the heart of the universe creates a fabric of meaning and wisdom and fosters new moments of mutuality for Earth and every species.

Roots of Engagement

An engaged cosmology will be rooted in a felt-sense of interdependence (contemplation), a desire that all peoples be free (liberation), and a reverence for a resacralized Earth (creation).

The Little Ones

Deep cultural therapy will focus on the nurture, support and protection of the little ones and unborn of every species. When we detach ourselves from the pain of the present moment, we experience an invitation to awaken the imagination of youth to provide both protection and a portal into the future.

Interrelatedness and Communion

The cultural worker is a builder of community. The work is nourished and energized by inseparability and the desire to commune with all members of the community of life – the "Noah's Ark of Existence." The cultural worker is drawn forth by longing to make belonging in the universe possible and dissolving the separation, exile, alienation or loneliness, that prevent authentic relationships with Soul, Life, Earth and the Divine.

Creative Energy and the Celebration of Uniqueness

The universe mirrors the divine act of creativity and participates in abundant acts of creativity and expressions of new life. Each person dances into the future with a unique capacity for creativity and celebration of new life.

A Cosmic and Cultural Convergence

We are supported by the ultimate powers of the universe as they make themselves present to us through the spontaneities within our own beings.

—Thomas Berry

An engaged cosmology will evoke and support the practice of generosity and big-heartedness. We realize deeply our interconnectedness. In a new moment of transformation we are inspired to work for the liberation of all, to "set the captives free."

An engaged cosmology accesses the emergent energy that breaks through and celebrates the beauty and exuberance of new life.

As we discover the dynamic connection between the "stars and the street" we realize that the energy released in the process has self-healing properties. This primal energy first found its expression in the originating energy of the universe. Today it becomes a cleansing and protective source to dispel all doubt and despair and makes it possible for beauty to blossom forth.

A beauty that is present in relationship, in difference and in depth. A beauty that blossoms forth in the land, in the soul of the people. A beauty that is present in the child, palpable in the elder, that envelopes the landscape and the soul. A beauty that draws us forward into a new moment of liberation, where we can sing with Nina Simone and so many others, "how it feels to be free!"

A beauty that shines forth like a blade of grass through broken pavement. A beauty that calls forth fresh moments of hope, that is "oxygen for the soul" and a "conviction that something makes sense, regardless of how it turns out."

A beauty that evokes the practice of an engaged cosmology, reminds us of our common origins and of the profound Paschal moments of Gethsemane and Easter.

A beauty that stirs the imagination and attunes us to hear the universal voice of vocation.

A beauty that invites us into a place of meaning, as we create together "unforgettable membranes of meaning" to nurture our journey and move us forward into the future.

A beauty that will nurture an engaged cosmology and empower us to transform the world through the balanced turbulence of intimacy and contemplation, mysticism and action.

A beauty that will invite us to celebrate new thresholds of possibility and hope, as we position ourselves at the doorway of

- Gratitude for the present
- Hope for tomorrow
- Appreciation of generosity
- Wonder of sacredness
- Alignment in wisdom

An engaged cosmology that unites the stars and the street will remind us of the deep connection between the universal wisdom revealed in the work of cultural transformation, and the dynamic powers present in the unfolding universe. When a dynamic integration occurs between these two powers, an engaged cosmology blossoms forth.

The Dynamics of Engagement

Engaged cosmology is the contextual and culminating action that flows from a reflection that views the longing of soul as contemplation of the interdependence of the universe; the longing of life as liberation of the entire earth community; the longing of earth as a celebration of the awe, wonder, beauty and pain of creation; and the longing of the Divine as the unspoken hunger for sacredness and depth that find expression in a spectrum theology of contemplation (soul), liberation (life) and Creation (earth) whose action is a verb that creates mutuality and alignment between the dynamics of the universe and strategic approaches to personal, social and ecological transformation.

The primary portals of our development as a people are marked by relationships: relationships to soul, life, earth and divine. When we understand that these relationships are deepened and empowered by the desire, love, attraction and longing that reside within the universe, we have entered the arena of an engaged cosmology.

Suddenly all divisions and dualisms are dissolved; all separations between religion and science, impulse and conscience, cosmology and culturel melt into a new-found oneness. We discover that all approaches and disciplines need each other; a fresh alignment between cosmic wisdom and the universality of cultural insight tumbles forth – we have discovered an engaged cosmology. The universal dynamics of cultural transformation and the principles operative in the universe coalesce into a new consciousness and new avenues of action.

Within this new-found fusion of cosmology and cultural action we discover great joy and the possibility of empowerment.

The dialogue between culture and cosmology will result in an architecture for change: an approach embedded in the cosmos, distilled from the theory and practice of deep cultural work and responsive to needs of this particular cultural moment.

An engaged cosmology will reduce the distance between the world as it is and the world as we would like it to be. It will heal the disparity between our vision of a new humanity and the dysfunctional world in which we live. The manifestation of an engaged cosmology will involve a continuing effort to discover the cultural implication of those tendencies that are deeply encoded in the human venture.

An engaged cosmology will involve the dynamic integration of all that is beautiful, mysterious and true. It will weave together into a harmonious tapestry the valued legacy of our religious traditions, the profound insights of the experience of soul, the practices of cultural transformation, and the mystery of the story of the universe. It will be out of the interaction and distilled wisdom of these cascading revelations that a new world of unprecedented beauty will be called forth. A world manifesting value, meaning and wonder mediated by the revelatory impact of a new master narrative – The Universe Story.

The understanding of the universe and the practice of geo-justice are constitutive to an engaged cosmology and integral to what it means to be human.

Last night as I slept
I dreamt – marvelous error
that it was my God I had here in my heart.

—Pablo Neruda

Engaged Cosmology

Conscious Action

Conscious action celebrates
Inclusiveness
Through integral gestures
Of Soul, Life, and Earth

Foundation for Prolonged Engagement

Years ago the Cursillo Movement was founded in Majorca, Spain. The purpose of this short course was to develop a deeper involvement among people in the life of the church.

A foundational principle for the Cursillo Movement was that to prepare people for the long haul (*ultreya*), three things were necessary: piety, study and action. They were visualized as three legs of a stool. For the stool to be stable and strong, each of its three legs needed to be fully functional.

Analogously, I suggest that three principles are necessary to insure a prolonged participation in Engaged Cosmology. These are

- Vision/Dream
- Engagement/Action
- Soul Work/Spiritual Practice

Vision/Dream

The vision/dream gains access to a profound urge that invites us to go further, to keep hope alive and cross the threshold into a better tomorrow. The vision/dream makes it possible to imagine how our world could be, to become receptive to those revelatory moments that alter and illuminate our lives. The vision/dream makes it possible for us to live in unprecedented ways. When we dream, we gain access to passion and compassion. We take our lives in our own hands and become deeply committed to do what needs to be done.

Engagement/Action

Through conscientious action we create culture and build a bridge into the new era that awaits us. We become visually literate, see the world as it is, and are committed to create a world as we would like it to be. Our action is guided by the lessons learned from cosmology and cultural transformation.

With Martin Luther King, Jr., we are convinced that "the arc of the universe is long and bends toward justice." Our action becomes a celebration of the interdependence of all things, freedom for all sentient beings and the primary revelation that is present everywhere in creation. Through conscious engagement we become poet and politician, infused with a renewed ability to act. Through reciprocity and trust we imagine and create a world where beauty can shine forth.

Soul Work/Spiritual Practice

Soul work challenges us to become transparent and fully present to life. We pay attention to existence and attune our lives to the unfolding dynamics of the universe. Through spiritual practice we gain courage and sustain our participation to create a better world: a world punctuated with dramatic moments of transformation and challenge that reveal and intensify the deep mystery that is operative in everyday existence, a world where we discover that our deepest longing comes from a cosmic and sacred source. Soul work is an expression of gratitude and a search for meaning.

Synthesis and Reflection

As we move forward into an engaged cosmology through the dynamic interaction of vision/dream, engagement/action and soul work/spiritual practice, we are mindful of the wisdom of the prophets of the past. Our acts of creativity and compassion cannot be confined to pre-ordained methods or prescribed tactics. Rather our approach is that every context is new, every challenge unique. The themes of engaged cosmology and the dynamics of dream, action and soul work are designed to focus and energize our efforts. These approaches represent a converging wisdom of cultural work and cosmological consciousness. They are guidelines for a future yet to be born.

Engaged cosmology will integrate consciousness and conscience, thought and action. This integral awareness will nurture a "theory and practice" approach. Our cosmological vision will find expression in collective action. Through awareness of the interdependence of all things (contemplation), the commitment to set all creatures free (liberation) and an intimate relationship with the natural world (creation), we set out to develop strategies for the important work that lies ahead.

In a world withering with the onslaught of terrorism, nuclear proliferation, military expansion, poverty for the many and affluence for the few, a new wisdom and activism is urgently needed – and longed for. The new synthesis of consciousness and action outlined in the contours of an engaged cosmology will support the prolonged participation required to embrace cosmic consciousness and take action in the world to heal what is broken and renew the face of the earth.

The process will be nurtured by a Trinitarian approach that has its basis in the spectrum theology of contemplation (soul work), liberation (action) and creation (dream), energized by the dynamics of the universe (interiority, differentiation and communion) and by the spirituality that flows from the experience of mystery, creativity and compassion.

Engaged cosmology nurtures an expanded horizon, a cosmic context whereby beauty and brokenness, creation and destruction, innovation and prolonged engagement, action and reflection, personal and cultural transformation, and cosmological powers, consciousness and conscience are woven into a seamless tapestry of soul, life, earth and divine to heal what is broken and renew the face of the earth as we embrace mystery, creativity and compassion.

Principles for Prolonged Engagement	Component of Spectrum Theology	Principles of the Universe	Spiritual Experience
Soul Work/ Spiritual Practice	Contemplation	Interiority	Mystery
Engagement/Action	Liberation	Differentiation	Creativity
Vision/Dream	Creation	Communion	Compassion

Pathways to Wisdom

The modern Western error is of framing the human story in tragic alienation from the unfolding story of the cosmos.

—Charlene Spretnak

An engaged spirituality cosmology draws on a wisdom that is both ancient and new. From the deep wells of tradition we gain access to the wisdom that resides in the recesses of the universe and our souls. Through engaged spirituality we penetrate the profound mysteries embedded in existence and made palpably present through symbol, myth and analogy. An engaged spirituality activates the imagination and reminds us of our kinship with all life and the beauty present in each relationship.

Engaged spirituality invites us to discover the membranes of meaning present in each new moment, to perceive each encounter as a threshold to sacredness. An engaged spirituality invites us to align our energies with the dynamics of an unfolding universe and to accomplish whatever needs to be done to nurture compassion and new life. An engaged spirituality creates a context for fresh pathways to wisdom that are mystical, poetic and profoundly interrelated.

A spectrum theology of contemplation, liberation and creation that names our relationship to soul, life, earth and divine within the context of the universe story informs an engaged spirituality.

Engaged spirituality empowers participants to accomplish whatever needs to be done and to make it possible for depth, freedom, beauty and compassion to shine forth. This practice will include

- Generosity and genuine interest in the well-being of all.
- The resurgence of fresh energy to make possible the manifestation of new life.
- A celebration of and communion with the divine that is present in all things.
- A realization that we are all shaped, formed and genetically coded for gratitude, and compassion, sacredness and depth.

Through an engaged spirituality we participate in meaningful action that is congruent with our world views, true to our vision of the future, aligned with the unfolding of our lives, creative and transformative for all participants and mutually enhancing for the entire community of life.

A Better Tomorrow

The Arc of the universe is long, but it bends toward justice.
—Martin Luther King Jr.

We live today in a time where society is marked by indicators of withering and decay, a time when institutions oppose their original purposes, a time when the efforts of good people with the best of intentions often produce the opposite of their intended results.

Generous people are being called to create a context of support where their destinies are not defeated, to build a bridge into the future. It will be a bridge of transition and change: a bridge of new eras, new paradigms and a new world view. It will be a time to create clusters of generosity where people gather and reflect on approaches that fulfill their deeper purpose and build a vibrant Earth community.

It is a time to evoke and articulate a vision of a better tomorrow, a time to compose and live out Beatitudes for the New Creation in order to heal and energize the wounds of soul, society, and earth.

Beatitudes for the New Creation

- Blessed are the contemplatives: they shall experience the longing of the soul.
- Blessed are the liberators: they shall experience the longing of life.

- Blessed are the "earthlings": they shall experience the longing of creation.

- Blessed are those who long for God: they shall experience the interdependence of contemplation, the freedom of liberation, the beauty of the new creation.

The Spirit Speaks

The spirit stirs
Words well up
They speak for themselves
Of many things.

Of sacred turbulence
Of wonder and surprise
Of awesome beauty
And the deepest aspirations of the heart.

Beauty beckons us
To suffer and rejoice
To allow the paradox of presence
To engage us all
And from agony and ecstasy
To see uniqueness born.

This is my surprise to you
This is my true joy
That beauty will be born
And that all you hope for will make you free.

Reimagining Our Future

We are prophets of a future not our own.

—Oscar Romero

Relationships and Self-Discovery

How are we related to life, to Earth, to the Divine? How do we discover where we are, to gain guidance for the future? How do we take up our roles to be leaders in the 21st century?

When our ancestors began their prophetic work with its particular challenges, the times were different and the Great Work of those moments unique to the time.

In the intervening years much has been accomplished in schools, projects of community development; hospitals and clinics have been initiated and community education and training programs are underway.

As we reflect on the legacy of the past, we ask, "What are our challenges today?" As we review the accomplishments of the past, we realize that there is much more to be accomplished.

- Wars have been won and lost.

- Land has been cultivated and cleared.

- Technology has given us great gifts and has also been instrumental in unimagined destruction.

- The industrial revolution has changed the world. Transportation has gone from the horse and buggy to jet planes; communication has moved from courier pigeon to e-mail; agriculture has moved from family gardens to agribusiness. Healthcare has changed from family doctors to state-funded delivery systems; education from two-room schools to distance learning and international student exchange; clothing has shifted from traditional habits to street clothes; religion from catechism to the cosmos; our region from a healthy environment and a land to a time of genocide, fertilizers and industrial agriculture; conflict among nations and peoples has shifted from spears to smart bombs, pre-emptive strikes and collateral damage.

We have moved from a time when our ancestors awoke in the morning and knew where they were, to a time of cultural Alzheimer's when people on the planet lose their way.

Today we are like the adopted young man in the northwest of the United States who, when he learned of his adoption, engaged in the task of discovering who his parents were. Today as a people we enter a new moment of grace, a time of possibility and promise, a time to nurture and to discover more mutually enhancing relationships between humanity and earth. We enter a time when we are working to discover our origins and direction into the future, our New Story.

Prophetic Roots

Amidst volcanic eruptions resulting in rigidity of structures and a metastasized culture, sometimes referred to as a culture of death, fresh energy and a new moment has come upon us. The wisdom of the ages inscribed in the illumination of the mystics and the discoveries of modern science have converged. Unlike our ancestors impacted by the industrial era, we are now discovering who we are. Humanity has awakened to its destiny and call.

The Intervening Years

Through the revelations of the Hubble telescope, the insights of Albert Einstein, the vision of Pierre Teilhard de Chardin, the ecological awareness of cultural historian and geologian Thomas Berry and the liberation theology of Ivone Gebara and Leonardo Boff, we are now able to locate ourselves in the great cosmic drama: we have discovered our story. It is a story told by a child, proclaimed by the beauty of creation. A story that enhances our faith traditions and becomes a new context for the great work we are called upon to undertake here at the threshold of the 21st century.

Contemporary Challenges

Our great work is revealed by the challenge to respond with courage and compassion to this unprecedented moment in human/ Earth history. Our call to the great work is born out of the wisdom of the medieval mystic Meister Eckhart, who named ministry as "whatever needs to be done." Our call today is to embody and celebrate the deep indigenous wisdom of aboriginal people whose presence on the land reveals the new story in magnificent ways.

Our call is to become instruments of health and wholeness; it is an invitation to heal both the planet and ourselves. It is a call for pure water, clean air, healthy livestock and a wholesome earth: a call to nurture and support the dignity of the child and the wisdom of the elder and to all of us who inhabit this sacred land. It is a call for wisdom and depth: a call to teach our children the wonders of creation, to invite each child to look to the stars and remind them that they behold the bonfire of their ancestors. A call to perceive in the poor and forsaken a special presence of the divine. It is a call to engagement, to an engaged cosmology; a call to retrieve and celebrate the wisdom of the entire community of life; a call to respond to the crises and challenges of our time, as we align our energy to the unfolding dynamics of the universe and become catalysts for justice in an uncaring world.

Catalysts for Justice

Here on the precipice of the new millennium we are invited to hear and respond to the call of justice: to connect the stars to the street, to comprehend the connection between the crack in the ozone layer and the crack sold in the street. It is an invitation to altruism and generosity. It is a time to transcend narrow self-interest and be enchanted by the generosity of the sun; a time for bigheartedness, when with magnanimity our hearts open and our imagination soars; a time of interconnectedness and inter-being. It is an invitation to experience freedom and volcanic eruptions of the soul as we set about letting all the captives free. An invitation to resurgence and regeneration where our collective work makes possible emergence, beauty and new life; an invitation to weave together a membrane of compassion that dispels despair and reignites the original fire, to illuminate the dark night of our cultural soul; an invitation to a deep resonance with all of life when, with all artists, we will share the profound experience of "how it feels to be free"; an invitation to celebrate and realize that hope is not a conviction that something will turn out well, but a deep certainty that something makes sense and is worth doing regardless of how it turns out.

Engaging with Cosmology

As we gaze upon the beauty resulting from the volcanic eruptions and the enchanting landscape of bushlands and beaches, of valleys and mountaintops, we ponder again the great History of the Universe and reflect on our common origin. From this place we know deeply that we are all shaped and formed in that same primordial furnace; we feel energized again, to endure the bitter and burdensome moments of life, the Gethsemane moments as we engage in the Paschal mystery story of our time, the life, death and rebirth of our people and our planet here in the beauty of God's creation.

Our invitation at this time is to realize again that our work is a significant paragraph in the great cosmic story, a story told in each of our lives and projects and heard daily through the stars and the streets. It is an invitation to awaken again to the realization that where we stand determines what we see, and that our position on this planet is to stand with the children and the poor of every species on this sacred Earth. We are here to celebrate a new invitation, to create membranes of meaning, and embrace a new cosmic vision that will include

- Imagination and wisdom
- Courage and engagement
- Intimacy and contemplation
- Trust and equanimity within the turbulence of new life.

A Vision for Tomorrow

We honour our ancestors, express gratitude for this present moment and look towards the future with anticipation and hope. It is a future inscribed in each of our hearts and punctuated by our participation in the great work, our participation in mission. It is a future incarnated in our commitment to partnership, participation and protection. It is a future that will be enhanced by our shared vision that nurtures dignity, identity and respect.

· A future that is energized by the awe and wonder of an unfolding universe. A future that honours and celebrates tenderness and strength, and is captured by the vision of a flower bursting through the concrete, to bring beauty to a place neglected and oppressed. We hold forth a vision that will be embraced in this new moment of justice when we will create the conditions among us for beauty to blossom forth. It is a new moment when each person, and each project will compose a sonnet of justice, a song of compassion, for

Earth and every species; each will become an instrument in the orchestra to intone the music of creation and a new chapter in the great story that calls us together.

The Arc of the Universe is long, but it bends towards justice.

—Martin Luther King, Jr.

A Sonnet to the New Wonderland

In the land of the Long White Cloud

Maori legends are told

In this sacred place

Volcanoes erupt as beauty shines forth.

In a deep dark forest

The endangered kiwi lives

While the warmth of land and people

Proclaims that all are welcome here.

—Ka Ora

A Great Resurgence

A resurrection spirituality is being born out of this cosmic paschal moment, a sign and the midwife of new life for the planet and its peoples. In El Salvador, the people have written *"Resurgemos"* on the hillside where so many lost their lives during the earthquakes of 2001. The Inuit of Canada are announcing it. It is rising from the poverty and pain of the Guatemalan people in Central America. It is coming to consciousness and nurturing life in Ireland and Australia, New Zealand, South Korea and across the United States and Canada. It is a resurging spirituality, empowered by an Easter energy, marked by a converging concern for the restoration of the earth, the restructuring of society and care of the soul.

Emerging from this paschal moment is a new perspective on relationship to soul, life, Earth and God; a new energy of freedom and fulfillment for the planet and every species. It is an energy generated by the reality of human suffering and planetary pain, an energy that sees cosmic significance in awakening to the presence of a starving child and the abused earth as the threshold of a new exodus event, a new moment of solidarity.

At this Easter moment the poor speak to us in many voices. As we listen to the cry of the poor and the cry of the earth, we begin to understand from a personal and a planetary perspective that the poor are the sacrament of God and they have lessons to teach us. Salvadoran theologian Jon Sobrino, SJ, writes:

> The poor transmit realities and values which are very difficult. To find, outside their world, hope instead of selfishness, community instead of individualism, celebration instead of simple amusement, creativity instead of culturally imposed mimicry, a sense of transcendence instead of the blunt pragmatism and positivism of other worlds.

The poor make up two thirds of the world's population; this demonstrates that the hallmark of our times is poverty. It follows that our capacity to live a preferential option for poor people and the poor earth is the starting point for a new and authentic spirituality: a spirituality that begins at the edge of our longings – the longings of Soul, Life, Earth, and God.

Revisioning Abundance and Belonging: Toward a Viable Future

Unspoken Hunger

At the heart of our spiritual journey resides the longing to belong and to live a meaningful and joyful life. Simultaneously, there springs up within the soul of our culture a profound aspiration to transcend limitations and embrace the mystery that is constantly in our midst. When we encounter the fault line between mystery and comprehension, many questions emerge. They invite us to reflect more deeply on the relationship between

- intimacy and contemplation
- engagement and detachment
- feminism and pro-male attitudes
- poetry and politics

- the Great Work and right livelihood
- our personal journey and the New Story
- mystical cosmology and the life of engagement
- vocation and living meaningfully in a dislocated culture
- spirituality and religion

Our journey toward a healthy, functional future requires an openness to new states of consciousness, to welcoming the unexpected in our lives, whether insights, actions or relationships. We are also invited to consider deeply the impact of a living cosmology (a new vision for life) that sees all of creation functioning in an interrelated, mutually enhancing and interdependent way. This perspective sheds light on our place in the unfolding drama of the universe. It is a world view that generates gratitude and fresh psychic energy for the challenges that lie ahead. We can understand this energy as a fire that burns deeply with passion and compassion to heal the wounds of the human and other-than-human world; an energy that evokes within us a new mystical cosmology that will become the ground for a fluid and fruitful integration of intimacy and contemplation – a crucible for a life charged with beauty, vision and divine presence. We will be enriched when we explore deeply the longing that penetrates our souls, our lives, our planet and the Divine.

It is commonly understood that crises can provide opportunity for change and assist us to move forward in new and unprecedented ways, to see things differently, and subsequently to act differently. As we look back upon the rubble of a post-industrial age, we begin to see what we have done and perhaps ask why we are here and what we are called to do in the face of a dangerous and hopeful future. The crisis of cultural degeneration invites us to engage in the work of transformation and become people with listening hearts. This work will nurture a renewed sensitivity and our capacity to take up the challenge of healing the tragedy that we have caused.

We will extend our awareness and compassion beyond the human, and generously respond to this particular moment of grace and opportunity for transformation. With a renewed sense of awe and wonder we work to transform the dominant cultural paradigm.

A New Vision of Belonging

Miriam Moore writes, "We have the potential and the longing to become increasingly more conscious and more compassionate." To realize this vision it will be necessary to allow the creative process to unfold in our lives so that we can give birth to the most authentic expression of ourselves. We will increase our receptivity to new ideas and new ways of acting, dare to embrace the future with an openness to difference and a sense of adventure, and regard change with a sense of anticipation. We will develop a reverence for the wisdom figures of yesterday and today: our ancestors, our elders, and those of our tradition who have become architects for a prophetic and mystical life.

As we develop a mystical and engaged cosmology of intimacy and contemplation and become increasingly open to the longing of our heart, we will grow in the conviction that each person is genetically coded for goodness and compassion. We will have an increased ability to integrate spirituality and good work. We will be able to honour creativity, and bring beauty and healing to the poor and suffering of the world. We will simplify our lives, increase our commitment to justice and expand our understanding of *belonging*.

Belonging is not a destination. Indeed, it spurs us on to new longings. One belonging leads to another, and another. Belonging moves us forward, deepens us, lures us into ever more profound experiences of belonging. Belonging is a process of mutuality. What we belong to also belongs to us. There is reciprocity in belonging, a oneness and unity. "Belonging" can be another word for "mysticism"; ultimate belonging is experienced in our relationship with the Divine. The poets and the prophets of the past and present talk about a restlessness, an incompleteness and an intense thirst quenchable only by a relationship with the Divine; this is the ultimate homecoming, the ultimate belonging.

One of the symptoms of our current dysfunctional cosmology is a sense of homelessness. I believe that, because on a deep psychic level we are unable to come home to our planet, we have been unable to heal the wound of homelessness that ravages our country. When we fall in love with our planet and the planetary community, we can extend our concern beyond ourselves to a culture of belonging – for the planet, for the people, for the plants, the animals, all expressions of life.

From such a mysticism morality will flow. Belonging nurtures a social and ecological responsibility. It gives birth to justice. "Compassion" is another word for "belonging." It's a reciprocal relationship with the *anawim*, the voiceless, the little ones of God. Belonging is a source of revelation; through our relationship with the other, with deep listening, we hear the voice of God and contact the divine. Belonging brings a fuller realization of our connection to the universe, to home, and to our place in the cosmos.

The Wonder and Awe of Oneness

Each of the classical traditions points us to a place of ultimate belonging: Nirvana, Heaven, Paradise – a state of mystical union. "Realized eschatology" is a theological term for letting heaven happen now, for making the future present in our midst in this moment. Science reveals that we live in a web of relationship, and that the cosmos itself is a place of belonging. This web of relationship is a pattern that connects us all. Belonging can heal the despair that stalks our culture and diminishes hope. When hope springs up in the soul, we become connected with life, with Earth and the Divine.

There is a connection between longing, belonging and chaos. The absence of belonging is longing. When we're in a state of longing, we're off-balance, because we're reaching for something, for a connection, a relationship, something to ground us, to root us. This chaotic state is uncomfortable and essential for change. The chaotic state is really the precursor of something opening up for us, to take us to another level, another place, another journey.

The longing or the be-longing that we experience is the capacity to deal with internal dislocation and the uncertainty about our traditions, our communities, and our lives. This uncertainty can be the energetic force that moves us to a new state of coherence. Change won't happen without dislocation – cultural dislocation, intrapsychic dislocation, relational dislocation. This new territory is often disturbing, dangerous and challenging. It is also refreshing, inviting and new; chaos is often the threshold to belonging. The capacity to embrace the instability of our existence, to hold it in community with friends, in our meditative reflective times, in our bodies, in our traditions and in our prayer, gives us the capacity to belong deeply in new ways. This movement toward belonging is beginning to happen.

Everyone, Everything, Belongs

The New Story and the cosmology that flows from it remind us that everything belongs in the universe. *Everyone* belongs. David Bohm is famous for saying, "There is no scientific evidence for separation." No *scientific* evidence. There's a lot of sociological and cultural evidence, but there's no scientific evidence. If we can allow the cosmology to truly seep into us, if we can meditate on belonging in the universe – we will experience belonging. There's a wonderful book by Fritjoff Capra and David Steindl-Rast by that very name, *Belonging in the Universe*. From their perspective, everything belongs. All of us belong. The trees belong. The puppies belong. The worms belong. The rain belongs. Everything is related and interconnected.

Consider the following situations: where is it possible that you didn't feel like you belonged? Take a few moments to reflect on what these questions evoke in you. You may choose to write, or draw, or sing as you ponder.

- Have you ever been in a country where you felt you didn't belong?
- Have you ever had an experience because of your ethnicity or your family history where you felt you did not belong?
- Have you ever had the occasion when you were confronted with a political situation where you felt alienated or at odds with those in power?
- Have you ever felt rooted in your own tradition and yet felt that you did not belong within that tradition?
- Have you ever felt that, because of your gender, you did not belong?

Now consider times when you did belong:
- Have you ever felt a sense of belonging through friendship?

- Have you ever felt a connection with the divine, God, source, spirit? Have you ever felt that you belonged to God?
- Have you ever felt that you belonged to your body, that you felt embodied, that you and your body belong to one another?
- Have you ever felt in your communities or educational experiences a sense of community and belonging?
- Have you ever felt that there was real meaning and purpose in your life, and that you belonged to a sense of destiny about your existence?

As you complete your reflection, focus briefly on two final questions:

- Where have you felt most that you belonged?
- What remains your greatest challenge?

The Voice of Our Calling

There is an enduring tension between belonging and the authentic self. One way of exploring this question is to trust the quantum leaps. There's a risk involved, of course – that's what is meant by "quantum leap." There's a time between departure and landing when one feels unsure whether there are any "air-traffic controllers" monitoring our leap. And yet it's thrilling when we burst out as our authentic self and find ourselves genuinely accepted, perhaps for the very first time.

To begin to live authentically from a functional cosmology will require that we experience a period of dislocation from the dominant culture. In other words, to live out of the new cosmology will make us less able to function in our dysfunctional world. To create a new world will require courage and commitment as we live in *this* world while simultaneously striving to change it. It will also require new structures of support during these "in-between" times.

Revisioning Roots

Where does religious tradition fit in our developing picture of creativity, belonging, wholeness and soul work? I return again and again to this question: "What is it that I believe?" Or, in the language of Sallie McFague, "What is my *credo*?" I often phrase this question

"What do I trust?" "Trust" is a better word than "believe" for this purpose: belief is cognitive, but trust is affective. When we ask, "What do I trust?" one way of finding an answer is to ask another question: "What is it that I'm not anxious about? What is it that doesn't make me nervous?" For each of us, there is a core conviction that grounds us, that is visceral and that is rooted in certainty. One of the challenges in dealing with our tradition is that sometimes our operative theology – our deep core convictions – seems at odds with our inherited tradition. The result is that we feel stifled and stuck.

As we have seen, through theological reflection, we can discover an alignment between the truth that is revealed in our hearts and what we have learned from our inherited traditions. It is a search for congruence. If we go deep enough into our own psychic passageways and deep enough into our tradition, we will meet that underground river which is the divine and there we will find the congruence of our operative theology.

Every Theology Is Contextual

An operative theology within the context of the universe story will make links between the new cosmology and our inherited tradition. On the basis that all theology is contextual, we ask where does the divine and the human fit in; what is the meaning of justice? In our questioning we are reminded that we must look at history from the point of view of those who suffer and are oppressed.

We are challenged also to realize that the energy for justice flows from our experience of the divine as encountered with humanity and the natural world. With this consciousness we appreciate how Francis of Assisi can speak of Brother Sun and Sister Moon. With this awareness, our vision with the universe, with creation and humanity becomes one experience of the divine.

The Evolutionary Role of Religion

Pierre Teilhard de Chardin wrote in his book *Activation of Energies*, "What is most vitally necessary to the thinking earth is a faith, a great faith, an evermore faith. To know that there's a way out, that there's air, and light, and love, and somewhere beyond the reach of all death. To know this is to know that it is neither an illusion nor a fairy tale." Teilhard challenges us: "It is there that we find what I may be so bold to call the evolutionary role of religion." The call of our generation is to discover the evolutionary role of religion.

Deep within the soul lies a longing for the Divine, a relentless longing, for a life that is fresh, new and original. This longing confronts us with choices and the promise of fresh hope and possibility as we strive to avoid the terrible risk of an unlived life. In our hunger for belonging we become increasingly enveloped in the mysterious presence of the divine.

Belonging happens when the longing of soul, life, Earth and the divine are quenched and responded to. Belonging happens when we are able to integrate intimacy and contemplation, communion and solitude, inwardness and the prophetic struggle, politics and mysticism, inner work and the analytical mind, soul work and community action, connection and interdependence, listening and recognition. Only when we view the world with "soul eyes" will we fashion a design for tomorrow. At the edge of our longing we discover a mystical and engaged cosmology to guide us into the days ahead.

The Search

Diving deep into the cosmic water of uncertainty, new frontiers of exploration beckon without answers or focused invitation.

Magnetic intuition draws me forth, into a gravitational adventure of the soul.

New-found engagement stirs deeply, in the uncertainty of the moment a shattering occurs.

As once, as if forever and yet for the first time, a cosmic vista emerges and unfolds.

Incarnation happens at the epicentre of my soul as I begin to understand at least for now and maybe later that I am a child of the universe, a child longing for wisdom and searching for home.

Longing to discover relatedness and the deep nurturing mystery that is the resource for connectedness and the resonating fire of my soul.

And so I wander, wander forth in search of meaning, purpose, passion and life.

Wander forth, in search of wonder and surprise.

Wander forth in search of balance, wisdom and a listening heart.

Wander forth in search of my place in an unfolding universe.

Wander forth in search of a new-found strength to struggle and discover within the recesses of my soul the "wellspring that I dare to call my life."

Wander forth in careless abandon, always giving notice that my place in the universe is contained in the seeds of all that I am, have been and will become.

All that has lead up to this moment, this galactic moment of wisdom and surprise, that cascaded into consciousness and culminated in the person that is me.

Those geological events that formed our planet home and now are the basis of our being.

Those incidents of new life that spring forth from the sea and flourish now on the hillside of our home.

Those momentous moments of fresh understanding that have become this gorgeous planet now newly conscious of celebrating itself.

And so the journey continues wrapped in an envelope of uncertainty embracing both hope and terror.

With a new-found vision of tomorrow and a peace that may never cease.

An Ecozoic Council

Real hope is an alternative networking.

—Diarmuid O'Murchu

A new era of mutually-enhancing human-earth relationships — a future dream of overcoming the limits and basic rhythms and conditions of technology.

—Steve Dunn and Anne Lonergan

From the edge of soul, life, Earth, and the divine, I imagine the possibility of an Ecozoic Centre and Council.

The Council will understand itself as a cosmic circle, open to fresh energy, the evolving nature of human consciousness and our collective call to participate in the Great Work.

The ethos of the Ecozoic Council and the Centre that holds its focus will be one of openness and deep listening.

The Ecozoic Centre will understand itself to be one of the many centres represented in the Council.

The Ecozoic Council's mission will be to

- Nurture and support a planetized consciousness, a cosmology that focuses on actions that are both global, local and personal.

- Support the ecologically affirming initiatives of globalization in regard to human rights and environmental work.

- Promote circles of shared wisdom, information, support and common action, whereby people and projects become aware of their unique contributions to the Great Work, and provide willing support for those who are engaged in diverse efforts.

- Provide the opportunity and context whereby participants in the council and their colleagues are able to reflect on and articulate an "operative cosmology" that will ground them in their personal journey, culture, tradition and the cosmos as they strive to engage in their contribution to the historical mission of humanity at this time.

Through listening deeply to each other and learning of the work to which we are called, members of the council will have the opportunity to see more deeply the uniqueness of their efforts and achieve an increased appreciation for the diverse yet global nature of our common task.

Through interaction and shared resources, participants will grow in the capacity to clarify and focus their strategies and action plans from each of the programs and projects represented in the circle.

Through dialogue and critical reflection, council participants will become collectively aware of the issues around which they share a common commitment and that can serve as a focus for a common action to energize and focus the council and the constituent groups whom they represent.

The Ecozoic Council and the Ecozoic Centre will provide an opportunity to raise our spirituality, cosmology and consciousness to a new level, and contribute to mutual enhancement through the interaction with every species in and through the Earth, while fulfilling the collective goal of preparing a better world for the children of every species.

Many years ago Archimedes said, "Give me a lever long enough and a place to stand and I will move the world." It is my hope that through the experience of sacredness and depth and the practice of engaged cosmology we may, in some small way, make our contribution to the world for which we long.

Following is an excerpt from a letter inviting participation in the Ecozoic Council.

Dear Friends of Sophia,

As a person of conscience and compassion we invite you to consider participation in the new Sophia Ecozoic Council being born among us this weekend. The Sophia Ecozoic Council will be a vehicle for information and support, a place of common action; a non-organization that will model the dynamics of the universe – each person, each project unique; an interconnected web of communication and communion with freedom and autonomy for everyone as we strive to make our personal and collective contribution to the Great Work. Become like the universe: autonomous, free, unique and connected.

Components of the Sophia Ecozoic Council:

INFORMATION – Bring awareness regarding people, written and recorded resources and programs, to people in your bio-region.

SUPPORT – Create relationships to assist you in continuing your participation in the Great Work through listening, wisdom circles and connection to movements and initiatives that parallel your vision and engagement.

COMMON ACTION – Align your actions with other individuals and groups to amplify the possibility of resolving issues and concerns for the sake of the planet and its peoples.

Our vision for the Sophia Ecozoic Council is that it will inspire a convergence of people who are active in the Great Work to develop unlikely coalitions that create the possibility for relationships with no external control and at the same time be a vehicle for people with shared values belonging to a vision larger than their own program.

(Note: Please refer to the Contact Information in the Appendix.)

Beatitudes for an Engaged Cosmology

Blessed are the hopeful: they hold a promise of tomorrow.

Blessed are the courageous: they embrace the challenge of today.

Blessed are the forgiving: they are free of the burden of the past.

Blessed are the people of prolonged engagement: they will create a better world for the children.

Blessed are the disappointed: they will rise and anticipate a better day.

Blessed are the self-forgetful: they will engage in a compassionate embrace.

Blessed are the flowers, bursting forth in the spring: they will bring beauty to the earth.

Blessed are the children, celebrating spontaneity and new life.

Blessed are the contemplatives: they will embrace the universe as one.

Blessed are the liberators: they will set all the captives free.

Blessed are the creation-centred: they will appreciate the awesomeness.

Blessed are the engaged mystics: they will ignite a fire on the earth and unite the stars with the street.

Divine/Contemplation/Liberation/Creation - Action/ Reflection

How has a deepened awareness of the emergent universe, of humanity's struggle for freedom and the recesses of our own soul prepared us to participate in an engaged cosmology? In light of a new understanding, what are your primary areas of concern for our planet here at the threshold of a new era? What actions do you plan to undertake to bring peace, joy and compassion to our world and every species?

If we long for God we long for the satisfaction and fulfillment of what we genuinely desire far and away beyond the titillating enticements of the market which have blocked the Wisdom to know.

—Mary Grey

Rediscovering the Divine

We rediscover the Divine as we

- Engage in collaborative projects that are marked by reciprocity, mutuality and a new level of community.

- Support personal and planetary challenges that are holistic and visionary, leading to passionate and practical action to bring balance to relationships and liberation to Earth and every species.

- Explore lifestyles that are increasingly congruent with the dynamics of the universe, that enhance an integral human presence, and find cultural expression in creativity, compassion and psychic depth that is ecologically aware, holistic and just, and born out of awe, wisdom and radical amazement.

- Discover and develop ways to engage in meaningful and collaborative action that is aligned to our world view and vision of the future, actions that are congruent with the narrative of our lives and the unfolding story of the universe that culminate in creativity and transformation infused with cosmological wisdom.

- Ponder deeply key questions that connect the heart of humanity to the heart of the cosmos to renew and inspire the soul as we prepare the transition into a new era of justice and planetary wisdom at this threatening moment in our history.

- Celebrate the three-dimensional journey that is personal, communal and cosmic; respond to those inclinations, hunches and intuitions that ignite our imaginations and summon us to engage in a spiritual journey grounded in our origins and marked by the touchstone categories of reciprocity, information, support and common action.

- Journey to the edge of our longing and heal our hunger for sacredness and depth as we create together a planetary community that is enveloped in courage, spontaneity and aspirations for good work.

A Blessing

Blessed is Earth
It shall flourish with radiant beauty.

Blessed are the waters
They will flow with clarity and quench our thirst.

Blessed are the trees
They shall absorb toxins
and give us breath.

Blessed are the birds
They shall soar stately in the sky.

Blessed are those in pain
They shall discover radiance in the dark.

Blessed are those who despair
They shall be enveloped in hopeful peace.

Blessed is the fire
It shall melt all walls and separation
with the energies of love.

Blessed are they who live in the universe,
are inclusive of all and celebrate the
resacralization of the planet
They shall experience beauty in all that
is revealed.

Epilogue

Our New Defining Moment

"We anticipate with great hope, a new creation adorned by songs of poets, imagination of artists, voices of prophets, hearts of healers, wisdom of mystics, fruits of creation, joy of children, and all those who listen with the ears of the soul and long for epiphanies at the edge of their unspoken hunger for sacredness and depth.

As we listen deeply to the invitation at this defining moment we respond to the challenge to integrate our longing with the experience of sacredness and depth, an experience that will heal all separateness – the spirit and the street, vision and despair, ritual and rigidity, a wounded heart and a gorgeous planet; a new vision, "soul eyes," through which we perceive and celebrate a vision, a story of interconnectedness and common action.

As we ponder this defining moment and anticipate the future, we take up the challenge to be, as Jean-Marc Elia says, "at the heart of things, of life, present where the future is in the process of being born, participating in its creation." Perhaps it is here that we will satisfy our longing and become a new people enveloped in a land of beauty, prompted by gestures of balance, harmony and peace.

Turning Toward Home

As we look to the future, in a sense we turn toward home. As Thomas Berry would say, it's like "riding a horse and buggy" and turning toward home. When we feel the horse drawn toward its destination; a fresh energy empowers its journey and we move at a more rapid and enthusiastic pace.

Such a "turning toward" will be a "second exodus," a time like that of the Copernican Revolution when humanity was freed of the illusion that the Earth was the centre of the universe and everything revolved around it. This second exodus will require new myths and stories – a new master narrative – a new geography of soul, life, Earth and the divine.

The days and moments ahead will require a "paschal mystery" moment: a profound letting go and dying into the world before us and the world view that we have known.

The new life that will emerge among us will be marked by the birth of a new world order – a new meta-religious understanding, a new perception of the divine, a new politics and economics, and a new meaning of peace.

This new transformation will be a rebirth that will call on and access both the creative and collective energy of the past, as well as the fresh visions and dreams being born in the hearts and minds of people today. A new meaning of love will be nurtured in the embrace of all those relationships that hold us together in this new world, this new web of life.

As we turn toward home and reflect on our origins, new images will emerge – images of hope for a better tomorrow – images that respond to our longing for sacredness and depth.

Images of Tomorrow

As we stand here at the edge of our longing, positioned at the threshold of sacredness and depth, images of tomorrow emerge into consciousness bringing a new vision of hope to a world immersed in anxiety.

Hope from a new vision of monastery whose architecture is created out of the dynamic relationships that are nurtured by the wonder of the universe and our place in the future.

Hope from a fresh vision of novitiate, where each person's cosmological imagination reveals what it means to be human in an unfolding universe.

Hope from a renewed sense of home, an experience whereby we are re-energized to heal the wound of homelessness, and become energized for the journey, like a horse who enthusiastically gallops when pointed toward home.

Hope from a gallery of beauty that touches every soul and reminds us of the gorgeous planet that invites us to commune and be at one.

Within this galaxy of images resides a unity, a healing oneness that unites point zero and ground zero, the crack in the ozone layer and the crack in the street, and all that is a manifestation of beauty to heal our longing for sacredness and depth.

At the close of a spring semester the students planted a small oak tree in the Peace Garden on campus. None of us will be there when that little sapling becomes a tall oak. Yet, without the planting, watering and care there will be no tall oak. The work of engaged cosmology is to plant trees and to keep alive a hope-filled promise of a better tomorrow.

Each of us is like a tree of life, with our roots placed deeply in the earth, giving birth to a new economic system of sustainability and diversity: a trunk of biocracy and a fully functioning democracy; branches of a meta-religious movement, an ecozoic council that supports, nurtures and motivates all initiatives toward a more mutually enhancing relationship with Earth; and leaves that represent the wisdom of all genders and traditions, and a deepening commitment to a preferential option for the earth.

> *Defenseless under the night, our world in stupor lies, yet dotted everywhere, ironic points of light flash out wherever the just exchange their messages. May I compose like them, of eros and of dust, beleaguered by the same negation and despair, show an affirming flame.*
>
> —W.H. Auden

Afterword

> *The educator (engaged cosmologist) is a politician and artist who must use the science of techniques but must never become a cold, neutral technician.*
>
> —Paolo Freire

The Journey

Some years ago I contemplated what I envisioned a sabbatical could be, the people and places I would visit and learn from to deepen and challenge my spiritual journey.

My first stop was to be Gethsemane Abbey in Kentucky, the home of Thomas Merton. There I would deepen my spiritual practice and reflect on the meaning of contemplation as described by Merton: "Contemplation is a deep awareness of the interdependence of all things."

From Kentucky, I would head to Peru to the Institute of Bartholome de las Casas to meet with Gustavo Gutierrez. Here I could see the truth of Brazilian theologian Ivone Gebara's words: "Liberation theology's greatest contribution was its refocusing attention on the plight of the poor as a fundamental theological issue and its encouragement of a spirituality centered on the struggle for liberation from its various oppressions, especially from so-called social sins."

My sabbatical journey would next return me to the United States to reflect on the new cosmology as articulated in the writings of Thomas Berry, at that time in residence at the Riverdale Center for Religious Research; Miriam MacGillis at Genesis Farm; Brian Swimme; Rosemary Radford Ruether; and many others. I wanted to live out Thomas Berry's description of "the planet earth with all its wonders [as] the place for the meeting of the divine and the human."

The Quest

The primary object of the story is the realization of wonder and delight.

—N. Scott Momaday

I now realize that my quest was prompted by a longing to explore my roots, a hunger to discover from within the recesses of my tradition and the wisdom of contemporary authors and prophets a spirituality that would empower me and my colleagues to make sense of the past and engage in the challenges of this critical moment in human/earth history.

Therapist of the Apathetic

I realize now, more clearly than I did then, that I was exploring my roots, striving to discover within the recesses of my Christian tradition a spirituality that would empower me to make sense of my past and come to grips with the present. The past four decades have been a time punctuated by profound change, great hope, thresholds of uncertainty, and an enduring desire to mine the wisdom and good work of those who had gone before. My imagination is stirred when I recall Vatican II with its promise of a democratized Church and the fulfillment of great expectations. The impact of the urban crisis, with its companions the civil rights movement and the Vietnam war, profoundly changed our lives and set many of us on new paths. It was this ethos of change, in the wake of these many cultural earthquakes, that drew me to the Industrial Areas Foundation Saul Alinsky Training Institute and the work of community organization. Alinsky writes, "It is this awakening of our people from the abysmal apathy that will awaken us to a sense of ourselves as members of a human family."

Vagabond of the Obvious

Soon after I left Chicago, I became aware of a prophetic voice speaking from a place of exile. Paolo Freire had been displaced from his homeland in Brazil and was based at the World Council of Churches in Geneva, Switzerland. His program of popular education was sweeping across the West, bringing critical reflection and transformative action to all who embraced his work. He wrote, "We cannot create knowledge without acting. The focus of action is to transform the world."

Pursuit of Self-Discovery

Profoundly impacted by the cultural turbulence, I entered therapy to explore the dynamics of my emotional life. I wanted to understand the personal and cultural impacts of my past and their effect on my efforts to be an agent of change. Later I was fortunate to meet the renowned psychiatrist Stan Grof and discover his approach to understanding the human psyche. His work was designed "to develop a new appreciation and reverence for all forms of life and a new understanding of the unity of all things...strong consideration of all humanity, compassion for all life." With the work of Grof my years of therapy took on a new meaning and my hoped-for sabbatical, though yet to be realized, took on new meaning as well.

From Barrios to Supernovas

By drawing on the wisdom and practice of the great cultural workers of the past and reflecting on their unique contributions within a cosmic context, we will be better able to fulfill our destiny and participate in the transformation of the world.

The great civil rights leader, Martin Luther King, Jr., realized the need for a clear strategy in order to engage in meaningful action from the perspective of a cosmic consciousness. As I reflected on what I now call "Spectrum Theology," the synthesis of contemplation, liberation and creation theologies from the perspective of the universe, I began to realize the seeds of an engaged cosmology – of that universal "Arc of justice" of which King spoke.

Contemplation reflects on the interdependence of all things and communes with cosmic forces to empower action. *Liberation* attends to the plight of the poor and shows us that our quest is for the freedom not only of humanity but of all creation. Creation presents the challenge to heal ecological devastation while celebrating the entire universe as "the place that bear's God's signature," manifest in the divine beauty and sacred mystery that is everywhere.

Components of an Engaged Cosmology – Insights and Revelations

In an engaged cosmology we awaken to the creative energy that streams through the cosmos. We understand that our role is to give this energy focus and expression. We fulfill our destiny and participate in the transformation of a broken world when we engage in this work.

Engaged cosmology reveals new insights into the great cultural workers of the past and present when we view their practice through the lens of the universe.

Engaged cosmology enhances our ability to act. We become aware that the creative energy of the universe is pulsating through our lives and activating every aspect of our being.

Engaged cosmology nurtures a critical reflection that gives expression to a deep cosmic longing that calls us to heal what is broken and transform the face of the earth as we strive to make all things new.

Engaged cosmology challenges us to transform our consciousness and our conscience. We are invited to weave together webs of wisdom and programs of action. As we honour the aspirations of the heart, we rediscover "the God of the Universe" and set our sails toward a hope-filled future.

A New Moment

As I describe the unfolding of a mystical and engaged cosmology, I realize a defining moment in my journey occurred when I named our personal and planetary challenge as the work of geo-justice. I spent years in community organization and development in Toronto and Chicago; at the same time psychotherapy captured my interest. I had also been introduced to a global perspective through the work of Jerry and Patricia Mische, co-founders of Global Education Associates, particularly their book *Toward a Human World Order.*

Through the work of Pierre Teilhard de Chardin and Thomas Berry, I discovered the components of geo-justice, which I called global, local and psycho-social. The vision is realized when these components were developed, and we experience a world of harmony, balance and peace. This vision became even more powerful for me when I discovered the resonance between these components and the dynamics of the universe itself:

- Global/Communion: Everything is related to everything else.
- Local/Differentiation: Nothing is the same as anything else.
- Psycho-Social/Interiority: Everything has personality and depth.

This naming and discovery of geo-justice made it possible to build a bridge between my cultural work and the dynamics of the universe as revealed in the New Cosmology.

As I pondered the deeper meanings of geo-justice, I began to understand the Trinitarian dimension in the following way:

- Communion = Spirit
- Differentiation = Creator
- Interiority = World

I also began to relate the components of geo-justice to spiritual practice:

- Global—Communion—Compassion
- Local—Differentiation—Creativity
- Psycho-Social—Interiority—Contemplation/Depth

A Turning Point

During our Sophia Summer Institute on Race and the Cosmos a new awareness came upon me. Even though I had built a bridge between culture and the cosmos, "The New Cosmology" still did not have a strategy!

I felt compelled to retrace my steps into my previous cultural work. I referred again to the writings of Saul Alinsky and Paulo Freire in particular. I also returned to the writings of Thomas Berry and others. I began to search for and discover parallel themes in their work. I was looking for connections between cultural work and the New Cosmology with the intention of strengthening cultural strategies of community organization and popular education with the words and power of the New Cosmology.

I was convinced that if I could connect the strategic approaches of cultural transformation to the parallel themes in the New Cosmology, the result would be what I now call "Engaged Cosmology" – an approach which would connect the wisdom of deep cultural work to the dynamic capacities that pulsate through the universe.

Rooted in Tradition

As I reflected on the emergence of a mystical and engaged cosmology in these pages, I was thrilled when I discovered the connections with my own religious tradition. The relationship of Soul to Contemplation, Life to Liberation, and Earth to Creation rooted this work in what I now call "Spectrum Theology," each dimension extending beyond the limits of its original definition to include a cosmological perspective, together culminating in an integrative process I have named "spectrum theology" that empowers both the mystical and the engaged dimensions of our journeys.

Our New Threshold Moment

This is and can be a "Second Genesis," a threshold in time, a defining moment, a new beginning. It is time for a new exodus as well: a moment to liberate our world views, cultural work and spiritual practice from the confinement of conformity and outmoded approaches. A mystical and engaged cosmology will embrace both the ancient and new, cultural and cosmic pathways to wisdom in order to heal our endangered planet and declining culture. An engaged cosmology will strive to make all things new, embrace the beauty of the present moment and the awe and wonder it brings to our lives.

This is a new moment when each person and each project will compose a sonnet of justice, a song of compassion for earth and every species. Each will become an instrument in the orchestra to intone the music of creation: to become a new chapter in the great story that calls us all together.

The Promise

Energy rises
Convergence in the sky
Collaboration happens
Culture becomes cosmic

Spontaneity bursts forth
Soul awakens
An energetic ocean
Pours forth onto humanity and earth.

Intimacy and contemplation abound
In the longing for mystery and communion
A search for parallel approaches
Reveals the promise of a better world.

Appendix

A Practice of Engagement

In light of the questions posed at the conclusion of each chapter, follow the procedure outlined below:

Create: a code, a visual and literal depiction that reveals how you are held back from achieving the themes outlined in each chapter. A code is *familiar* (inside people's experiences), *involving* (evokes response), *generative* (emerges from lived experience), and *relational* (connects us to others).

As you reflect on this theme and create this depiction, ponder the following questions:

- What holds you back?

- What gets in the way?

- What stands between you and the fullest expression of freedom for yourself, others and the other-than-human world?

Reflect personally and collectively on the code in the following ways:

- What do you see? What do you feel?

- What encounters with people and the other-than-human world have deepened your experience of oppression and evoked a desire to liberate yourself, the oppressed peoples of the world, and the planet as well?

- What do you know about this code from personal experience?

- What is the group's experience of this theme?

- What are the historical/cultural/traditional underpinnings of this theme?

- What further understanding and experience of this theme do you intend to explore?

Toward a Spectrum Theology

Engaged Cosmology explores the operative dynamics present in contemplative, liberation and creation theologies and nurtures a resacralized world of harmony, balance and peace through geo-justice (the translation of the principles of differentiation, communion and interiority into cultural form), and the alignment of the powers of the cosmos with approaches to cultural transformation (personal, social and ecological).

Component	Approach	Description
Longing of Soul	Contemplation	Integrates your life through an awareness and awakening to one's interior life to more deeply penetrate the mystery of the interdependence of all things.
Longing of Other	Liberation	Nurtures critical reflection on humanity's relationship to the world for the sake of transformation.
Longing of Earth	Creation	Celebrates the new cosmic story, an awakened mysticism and the awesome beauty of creating art, culminating in compassion and justice.
Longing of the Divine	Mystical and Engaged Cosmology	Promotes a dynamic relationship between contemplation, liberation and creation that results in aligning the powers of the universe with the dynamics of cultural transformation.

Principles of an Engaged Cosmology

- Generosity and self-transcendence
- Restorative properties and the self-healing resurgence of the soul
- Evolutionary freedom within a vast unfolding universe to liberate the planet, oppressor and oppressed

- Within the volcanic eruptions present in the heart of the cosmos and the human heart we are guided by a mindful and sacred universe.

- Celebration of sacredness and culture – moments of divine presence.

- An unfolding universe and a future of gratitude, hope, beauty, wisdom always at the threshold of something new.

- The Great Story and the transformational events of our lives told both by the stars and the street that weave together membranes of meaning.

- Cosmic creation and destruction embedded within the Bethlehem, Gethsemane and Easter moments of grace.

The Practice of Engaged Cosmology

Principles for Prolonged Engagement	Component of Spectrum Theology	Principles of the Universe	Spiritual Experience
Soul Work/ Spiritual Practice	Contemplation	Interiority	Mystery
Engagement/Action	Liberation	Differentiation	Creativity
Vision/Dream	Creation	Communion	Compassion

We look toward the future with gratitude for those on whose shoulders we stand. Our hearts are stirred and our souls awakened to the awe and wonder of the universe. A new consciousness permeates our souls. We feel inspired, alive. We act in new ways.

This new awareness also presents a challenge – how to translate our new consciousness into concrete strategies for change.

To meet this challenge will require a commitment to preserve the integrity of the new cosmology and the consciousness that accompanies it; at the same time we develop approaches to apply this new awareness to concrete strategies for change.

Developing a Practice

The practice of an engaged cosmology will be developed within the context of a base community. Here participants will gather to pose questions, explore their deepest longing and listen attentively to one another. As they examine their responses in light of their spiritualities of contemplation, liberation and creation, they will be moved into action.

I propose that the sequence and focus of these base community gatherings should follow the order of the chapters of this book, and that the questions discussed include

Longing of Soul

What thresholds of sacredness and depth have been most helpful in your process (e.g. listening, remembering, letting go, heeding the prophets, practising compassion, relating to the little ones, honouring creation, envisioning)?

How has your reflection on these themes expanded your capacity to penetrate the mystery of existence?

What actions will enhance your ability to respond to the longing of soul and contribute to the awakening of your interior life?

Longing of Life

What encounters with a person or group (e.g. illness of self or a loved one, people of justice, poverty, war or political conflict) have opened your life to a deeper embrace of the mystery and meaning of life?

How have these moments of intimate connection with others transformed the nature of your relationships and reconstituted your perception of the world for the sake of transformation?

What action are you prompted to engage in to heal, strengthen and transform your relationships with others in the world?

Longing of Earth

What experiences with creation do you recall that have shaped and influenced your life? Have you participated in an ecology group such as Brothers of Earth or the Oblate Ecological Initiative?

How has your experience of the natural world awakened in you a sense of sacredness, appreciation of beauty and feelings of compassion?

How will you respond to the ecological devastation of our time? What actions can you take to resacralize the Earth?

Longing of the Divine

How can we become empowered to respond to the needs of this particular moment within the context of an emergent universe, with attention to the revelatory awareness of the interior life, the human struggle for authentic freedom, and a growing consciousness that all our experiences are connected and sacred?

How has your world view and religious tradition prepared you to be critical of and responsive to this particular moment of grace?

What actions does a mystical and engaged cosmology prompt you to undertake to bring peace, joy and compassion to our world?

A Time Alone

A time alone to ponder
purpose, place, and me.

A time alone to ponder
What will be revealed to see.

A time alone to ponder
The book that is my hungry soul.

A time alone to ponder
The beauty of a rose.

A time alone to ponder
My longings at the edge.

A time alone to ponder
The universe and its call.

A time alone to ponder
What it means just to be.

A time alone to ponder
The unspoken sacredness of life.

Contact for Sophia Center and the Ecozoic Council:

Sophia Center in Culture and Spirituality
Holy Names University
3500 Mountain Blvd.
Oakland, CA 94619
USA

Phone: 1-510-436-1046
Fax: 1-510-436-1338
E-mail: sophiactr@aol.com
Web site: www.hnu.edu/sophia

Sources

Prologue

- *Rilke's Book of Hours: Love Poems to God.* Anita Burrows & Joanna Macy, trans. New York: Riverhead Books, 1996, p. 88.
- "The Guardians" from Bread & Roses Residence at Genesis Farm Learning Center, Blairstown, NJ.
- Rabbi Abraham Heschel, quoted by Rev. Liza Ranchow at Sophia Center, October, 2003.

Chapter 1: Longing of Soul/Contemplation

- Robert Bellah. *Habits of the Heart: Individualism & Commitment in American Life.* Robert Bellah, Richard Madsen, William Sullivan, Ann Swidler, Steven Tipton. San Francisco: Harper & Row, 1985.
- Robert Bellah, Richard Madsen, William Sullivan, Ann Swidler, Steven Tipton. *The Good Society.* New York: Knopf, 1991.
- Thomas Berry, from the Introduction to *Soul Craft: Crossing into the Mysteries of Nature & Psyche,* by Bill Plotkin. Novato, CA: New World Library, 2003.
- Br. David Steindl-Rast, OSB. *The Music of Silence: Entering the Sacred Space of Monastic Experience.* San Francisco: Harper, 1995, p. 17.
- David Steindl-Rast, OSB. *Words of Common Sense: For Mind, Body and Soul.* Radnor, PA: Templeton Foundation Press, 2002.
- Thomas Merton. *The Inner Experience: Notes on Contemplation.* San Francisco: Harper, 2003.
- John O'Donohue. *Eternal Echoes: Exploring Our Yearning to Belong.* New York: Harper Collins, 1999.
- Rosemary Radford Ruether. *Introduction to Goddesses and the Sacred Feminine: A Western Religious History* (unpublished manuscript). Berkeley, CA: University of California Press, 2004.

- Leonardo Boff. *Cry of the Earth, Cry of the Poor.* Maryknoll, NY: Orbis Books, 1997.
- McGregor Smith in Collaboration with the Earth Literacy Network – Environmental Ethics Institute. *Earth Literacy: An Ethical/Spiritual Model of Education for the Ecological Crisis* (unpublished manuscript). Miami.
- Ursula King. *Christian Mystics: The Spiritual Heart of the Christian Tradition.* New York: Simon & Schuster, 1998.
- Mary Oliver. *New & Selected Poems.* Boston: Beacon Press, 1992, pp. 110, 114.
- Edward Schillebeeckx. *On Christian Faith: The Spiritual, Ethical and Political Dimensions.* New York: Crossroad, 1987.
- John Shea. *Gospel Light: Jesus Stories for Spiritual Consciousness.* New York: Crossroad, 1998.
- Thomas Merton. *Seeds of Contemplation.* New York: Dell, 1949, p. 21.
- Elizabeth Johnson, CSJ. *Women, Earth, and Creator Spirit.* Mahwah, NJ: Paulist Press, 1993.
- David Whyte. *Crossing the Unknown Sea: Work as a Pilgrimage of Identity.* Riverhead, NY, 2001.
- Stan Grof, *Psychology of the Future.* Albany, NY: State University of New York Press, 2000.
- Paulo Coelho. *Awakening Universe, Emerging Personhood.* Wyndham Hall Press, 2002.
- Thomas Moore. *The Soul's Religion.* New York: HarperCollins, 2002.
- John Yungblut. *The Gentle Art of Spiritual Guidance.* New York: Continuum, 1995.
- Kirk Schneider. *Rediscovering Awe, Splendor, Mystery and the Fluid Center of Life.* St. Paul, MN: Paragon House, 2004.

Chapter 2: Longing of Life

- Ivone Gebara. *Longing for Running Water: Ecofeminism and Liberation.* Minneapolis, MN: Augsburg Fortress, 1999.
- Ivone Gebara. *Out of the Depths: Women's Experience of Evil and Salvation.* Minneapolis, MN: Fortress Press, 2002.

- Gregory Baum and Robert Elsberg, eds. *The Logic of Solidarity: Commentaries on Pope John Paul's II Encyclical "On Social Concern."* Maryknoll, NY: Orbis Books, 1989.

- Albert Nolan, OP. *To Nourish Our Faith: Theological Reflections on the Theology of Liberation.* London, UK: CAFOD, 1989.

- Gustavo Gutierrez. *The Green Bible.* Stephen Scharper and Hilary Cunningham, eds. Maryknoll, NY: Orbis Books, 1993.

- Gustavo Gutierrez. *The Theology of Liberation.* Maryknoll, NY: Orbis Books, 1984.

- Saul Alinsky. *Rules for Radicals.* New York: Random House, 1971.

- Saul Alinsky. *Reveille for Radicals.* New York: Vintage Books, 1969.

- Paulo Freire. *The Paulo Freire Reader.* Ana Maria Araujo Freire and Donald Macedo, eds. New York: Continuum, 2000.

- Jim Forest. *Love is the Measure: A Biography of Dorothy Day.* Maryknoll, NY: Orbis Books, 1994.

- Mary Oliver. "In Blackwater Woods" in *New and Selected Poems.* Boston: Beacon Press, 1992, p. 177.

- Mark Twain's essay quoted in Parish Bulletin, St. Joseph the Worker Church, Berkeley, CA, October, 2001.

- Marie Dennis, Renny Golden and Scott Wright. *Oscar Romero: Reflections on His Life and Writings.* Maryknoll, NY: Orbis Books, 2000.

- Albert Nolan, OP. *God in South Africa: The Challenge of the Gospel.* Grand Rapids, MI: Eerdmans, 1988.

- Thomas Berry. *The Dream of the Earth.* San Francisco: Sierra Club Books, 1988.

- Jim Forest. *Living with Wisdom: A Life of Thomas Merton.* Maryknoll, NY: Orbis Books, 1999.

- Leonardo Boff. *Cry of the Earth, Cry of the Poor.* Maryknoll, NY: Orbis Books, 1997.

- Gregory Baum. *Essays in Critical Theology.* Kansas City, MO: Sheed & Ward, 1994.

- Paulo Freire. *Pedagogy of the Heart.* New York: Continuum, 1997.

- Paulo Freire. *Pedagogy of Freedom: Ethics, Democracy and Civic Courage.* New York: Rowan & Littlefield, 1998.

- Gregory Baum. *The Twentieth Century: A Theological Overview.* Ottawa: Novalis, 1999.
- Leonardo Boff. *Ecology and Liberation.* Maryknoll, NY: Orbis Books, 1995.
- The Official Report of the Human Rights Office, Archdiocese of Guatemala. *Guatemala: Never Again!* Maryknoll, NY: Orbis Books, 1999.
- Benjamin Smillie. *Beyond the Social Gospel.* Toronto/Saskatoon: United Church Publishing House/Fifth House, 1991.
- Gail Straub. *The Rhythm of Compassion: Caring for Self, Connecting with Society.* Boston: Journey Editions, 2001.

Chapter 3: Longing of Earth

- *Rilke's Book of Hours: Love Poems to God.* Anita Burrows and Joanna Macy, trans. New York: Riverhead Books, 1996.
- Leonardo Boff. *Cry of the Earth, Cry of the Poor.* Maryknoll, NY: Orbis Books, 1997.
- Thomas Berry. *The Great Work.* New York: Bell Tower, 1999.
- Sallie McFague. *Life Abundant: Rethinking Theology and Economy for a Planet in Peril.* Minneapolis, MN: Fortress Press, 2001.
- Pierre Teilhard de Chardin. *The Human Phenomenon.* Sarah Appleton-Weber, trans. Portland, OR: Sussex Academic Press, 1999.
- Thomas Merton. *When the Trees Say Nothing: Writings on Patience.* Kathleen Deignan, ed. Notre Dame, IN: Sorin Book, 2003.
- James Carroll. *Toward a New Catholic Church: The Promise of Reform.* Boston: Houghton Mifflin, 2002.
- Thomas Berry. *The Dream of the Earth.* San Francisco: Sierra Club Books, 1988.
- Pierre Teilhard de Chardin. *Hymn of the Universe.* New York: Harper Torch Books, 1961.
- Jim Wallis. Notes from Call to Action Conference. Milwaukee, WI.
- Oriah Mountain Dreamer. *The Invitation.* San Francisco: Harper, 1999.
- Pierre Teilhard de Chardin. *Building the Earth.* New York: Avon Books, 1965.

- Leonardo Boff. *Ecology and Liberation.* Maryknoll, NY: Orbis Books, 1995.
- Susan Clayton and Susan Opotow, eds. *Identity and the Natural Environment.* Boston: Massachusetts Institute of Technology, 2003.
- Neil Darragh. *At Home in the Earth.* Auckland, NZ: Accent Publications, 2000.
- M.J. Zimmerman. *Trusting the Universe: A Journey of Reconnection and Healing.* Unpublished Ph.D. dissertation.

Chapter 4: Longing of the Divine

- *Rilke's Book of Hours: Love Poems to God.* Anita Burrows and Joanna Macy, trans. New York: Riverhead Books, 1996.
- Elizabeth Johnson, CSJ. *Women, Earth, and Creator Spirit.* Mahwah, NJ: Paulist Press, 1993.
- Elizabeth Johnson. *Friends of God and Prophets.* New York: Continuum, 1998.
- John O'Donohue. *Divine Beauty: The Invisible Embrace.* New York: Bantam, 2004.
- David Steindl-Rast, OSB. *A Listening Heart.* New York: Continuum, 2000.
- Saul Alinsky. *Rules for Radicals.* New York: Random House, 1971.
- Saul Alinsky. *Reveille for Radicals.* New York: Vintage Books, 1969.
- Thomas Berry. *The Dream of the Earth.* San Francisco: Sierra Club Books, 1988.
- Thomas Berry. *The Great Work.* New York: Bell Tower, 1999.
- Brian Swimme and Thomas Berry. *The Universe Story.* San Francisco: Harper, 1992.
- Charlene Spretnak. *Missing Mary: The Queen of Heaven and Her Re-Emergence in the Modern Church.* New York: MacMillan, 2004.
- Jon Sobrino. *Spirituality of Liberation: Toward Political Holiness.* Maryknoll, NY: Orbis Books, 1990.
- Ernesto Cardinale. *Cosmic Canticle.* Willimantic, CT: Curbstone Press, 1993.